Selina Schuster

An Analysis of Childhood and Child Labour in Charles Dickens' Works

David Copperfield and Oliver Twist

Anchor Compact

Schuster, Selina: An Analysis of Childhood and Child Labour in Charles Dickens'
Works: David Copperfield and Oliver Twist. Hamburg, Anchor Academic Publishing
2014
Original title of the thesis: Working-class Childhood and Child Labour in Victorian
England

Buch-ISBN: 978-3-95489-222-8
PDF-eBook-ISBN: 978-3-95489-722-3
Druck/Herstellung: Anchor Academic Publishing, Hamburg, 2014

Bibliografische Information der Deutschen Nationalbibliothek:
Die Deutsche Nationalbibliothek verzeichnet diese Publikation in der Deutschen
Nationalbibliografie; detaillierte bibliografische Daten sind im Internet über
http://dnb.d-nb.de abrufbar

Bibliographical Information of the German National Library:
The German National Library lists this publication in the German National Bibliography.
Detailed bibliographic data can be found at: http://dnb.d-nb.de

All rights reserved. This publication may not be reproduced, stored in a retrieval system
or transmitted, in any form or by any means, electronic, mechanical, photocopying,
recording or otherwise, without the prior permission of the publishers.

Das Werk einschließlich aller seiner Teile ist urheberrechtlich geschützt. Jede Verwertung
außerhalb der Grenzen des Urheberrechtsgesetzes ist ohne Zustimmung des Verlages
unzulässig und strafbar. Dies gilt insbesondere für Vervielfältigungen, Übersetzungen,
Mikroverfilmungen und die Einspeicherung und Bearbeitung in elektronischen Systemen.

Die Wiedergabe von Gebrauchsnamen, Handelsnamen, Warenbezeichnungen usw. in
diesem Werk berechtigt auch ohne besondere Kennzeichnung nicht zu der Annahme,
dass solche Namen im Sinne der Warenzeichen- und Markenschutz-Gesetzgebung als frei
zu betrachten wären und daher von jedermann benutzt werden dürften.

Die Informationen in diesem Werk wurden mit Sorgfalt erarbeitet. Dennoch können
Fehler nicht vollständig ausgeschlossen werden und die Diplomica Verlag GmbH, die
Autoren oder Übersetzer übernehmen keine juristische Verantwortung oder irgendeine
Haftung für evtl. verbliebene fehlerhafte Angaben und deren Folgen.

Alle Rechte vorbehalten

© Anchor Academic Publishing, ein Imprint der Diplomica® Verlag GmbH
http://www.diplom.de, Hamburg 2014
Printed in Germany

Table of Contents

1. Introduction 7
2. The Perception of Childhood and Child Labour in Victorian Britain 9
   2.1 The Middle-class – A romanticized Idealization 11
   2.2 The Working-class – The economic Factor of Child Labour 13
3. A Comment on Victorian Society - The Representation of Childhood and Child Labour in Charles Dickens' Novels 16
   3.1 Oliver Twist 16
      3.1.1 Orphans and the Workhouse 17
      3.1.2 Apprenticeship and Child Labour 19
      3.1.3 Thieves and Prostitutes 23
   3.2 David Copperfield 28
      3.2.1 Child Labour in Factories 29
      3.2.2 Debtor's Prison 32
      3.2.3 Fallen Women 33
   3.3 Dickens' Critique 36
4. Health and Safety Concerns 43
   4.1 Accidents and Dangers at Work 43
   4.2 Work related Diseases and long term Effects on Life Expectancy 44
5. Contemporary Perception of Child Labour 46
6. Political Countermeasures against Child Labour 49
   6.1 The Factories Act of 1844 49
7. Conclusion 52
8. List of Literature 54

1. Introduction

'When the empty bottles ran short, there were labels to be pasted on full ones, or corks to be fitted to them, or seals to be put upon the corks, or finished bottles to be packed in casks. All this work was my work, and of the boys employed upon it I was one. [...] As often as Mick Walker went away in the course of that forenoon, I mingled my tears with the water in which I was washing the bottles, and sobbed as if there were a flaw in my own breast, and it were in danger of bursting.'[1]

This citation taken from Charles Dickens' novel 'David Copperfield' impressively exemplifies a very important aspect of British history and the history of The Industrial Revolution in general. The time which is nowadays mostly associated with great progress, rising productivity rates, mass production and a general advancement in terms of science and technology was to large extends based upon the cheap and disposable manpower of children and young adults who 'between 1800 and 1850, [...] helped make Britain's economy the most advanced in the world.'[2] As Marjorie Cruickshank puts it in her book 'Children and Industry' child labour was ubiquitous in Victorian England: 'They [the children] were visible everywhere in the crowded thoroughfares as sweepers, beggars, and pickpockets. They were part of the mass of labourers in the workshops, factories and brickfields.'[3] With regard to this estimation the following work will deal with the description of working-class childhoods and child labour in Victorian England as they are presented in Charles Dickens' novels 'David Copperfield' and 'Oliver Twist'.

How was the life and work of children during the climax of the first phase of the Industrial Revolution like? Which aspects of childhood were Dickens describing in his novels and were his depictions close to reality or did he rather rely on artistic exaggeration? In order to answer these questions the first part of this work will deal with the Victorian perception of childhood in general before it focuses on the portrayals of children and childhood which Dickens has immortalized in his works. There will be a closer look at the perception of childhood during the time in which the novels are taking place, which roughly relates to the first decade of Queen Victoria's reign from the late 1830's to the early 1850's. The question is how children were perceived by the Victorians and how the phenomenon of increasing child labour did fit into this particular perception. Afterwards, there will be an examination of how the childhood experiences of children varied in regard to their different social classes.

---

[1] Dickens, Charles: *David Copperfield*, p.135f.
[2] Frost, Ginger: *Victorian Childhoods*, p.66.
[3] Cruickshank, Marjorie: *Children in Industry - Child health and welfare in North-West textile towns during the nineteenth century*, p.3.

After this general overview of childhoods, an analysis of Dickens' novels in regard to his depictions of these aspects as well as the descriptions of establishments which dealt with orphaned or impoverished children like the workhouse will follow. The results of this analysis will be related to secondary literature as well as to Dickens' own childhood experiences by taking a short look at his biography. Hence, the foremost important question emerges: what did Dickens want to achieve by making thieves, prostitutes and impoverished working-class boys his main characters and what were his aims in writing about such topics at all?

Following this analysis, the second part of the term paper will deal with the health and safety concerns which arose from the occupation of young adults and children in heavy manual labour and the poor living conditions of many working-class children in the areas of industrial concentration. What were the dangers the children were exposed to and how were the working conditions affecting their general health and life expectancy? Keeping these questions on safety at work in mind there will be a short look at countermeasures taken to prevent young children from working long hours in hazardous environments. As an example of political intervention on the topic the last part of this work will take a closer look at 'The Factories Act' of 1844 in order to decide whether the actions taken by the British government were sufficient and effective. This example also illustrates the contemporary perception of working children by the Victorian society. What were Dickens' contemporaries thinking about child labour? Did they share his views and criticism?

Aside from the primary sources provided in form of Charles Dickens' novels 'David Copperfield' and 'Oliver Twist', this term paper will rely to great lengths on the secondary literature 'Children and Industry' by Marjorie Cruickshank, 'Victorian Childhoods' by Ginger Frost, 'Childhood and Child Labour in the British Industrial Revolution' by Jane Humphries and 'Child Labour in Britain, 1750-1870' by Peter Kirby.

2. The Perception of Childhood and Child Labour in Victorian Britain

The Industrial Revolution was a time of enormous change for the British society. Science and technology developed rapidly and brought wealth and improvement into many sectors of life; inventions like the steam engine, power looms, the spinning jenny or the expansion of the road and rail network made life easier. But on the other hand it was also the time of great misery, exploitation and tremendous class differences between a very thin and very wealthy upper-class, a rising middle-class and a very broad and to a great extent extremely impoverished working-class.[4] Despite the fact that from the 1820's onwards the British economy expanded to become the richest in the world[5], which meant that Britain as a country became richer and richer, many working-class families did not benefit from these improvements at all.[6]

During the early part of the Victorian Age only two percent of the population formed the upper-class, which consisted of aristocrats and landed gentry whose most distinctive feature was the fact that its members didn't have to work for a living but relied on rental revenues and the income of investments made instead. The middle-class formed roughly 15 % of the population and consisted of those who ran their own businesses, like factory owners or were professionals like teachers, surgeons or lawyers. The remaining majority of 73 % of the population was considered as the working-class, whose members were working for wages and were paid weekly or monthly.[7] It is important to mention that there was an internal distinction between skilled and unskilled workers within this social class. Skilled workers had learned a trade and therefore made better wages than the vast group of unskilled workers who had nothing but their physical strength to put into the balance.[8] Whilst the middle-class earned the most from the developments of the time (from approximately 15 % of the population in 1815 it grew to 25 % by the turn of the century) the working-class fell by the wayside. Due to rapid urbanization, cities became large, densely populated and hopelessly overcrowded in a short period of time. The results were that whole districts of greater cities deteriorated and became slums like the East End of London which Dickens impressively describes in his novel 'Oliver Twist'.

---

[4] Frost, Ginger: *Victorian Childhoods*, p.1.
[5] Steinbach, Susie: *Understanding the Victorians,* p.77.
[6] Cf. Steinbach, Susie: *Understanding the Victorians*, p.84.
[7] Frost, Ginger: *Victorian Childhoods*, p.2.
[8] Cf. Frost, Ginger: *Victorian Childhoods*, p.3.

The Victorian Age was a very ambiguous time with great prosperity and terrible poverty going side by side. This ambiguity also becomes apparent in the perception of children and childhood. On the one hand children were estimated as immensely important and childhood was a heavily idealized and romanticized time – children were seen as sweet, little angels who were entirely good and innocent since they weren't corrupted by the cruel world yet. Herbert Tucker even calls it an 'obsession' when he says that 'never before had childhood became an obsession within the culture at large – yet in this case 'obsession' is not too strong a word.'[9] But on the other hand, despite this obsession with children, the child mortality rate, especially in poorer districts of great cities, was appallingly high[10] and child labour was a regular occurrence 'in a society in which child labor provided an opportunity for additional income for hard-pressed families and capital advantage for eager employers.'[11] Although children had already been working before the rise of the Industrial Revolution, during 'the early part of the nineteenth century, child labour became to be used on a scale it had never been used on before'[12], mainly for the simple reason that steam power and new machinery allowed children to take over work that had previously required the strength of grown men. 'The Industrial Revolution heralded in a change of form of child labour'[13] because it opened new ways to employ children in sectors which formerly had been virtually out of limits for a child's work capacity.

Taking all these facts into account it is an interesting observation that the children of the middle and upper-classes were adored and idolized while their poor fellows were exploited and neglected by the same society that claimed to love children above all else. It is a fact that 'the quality of daily life in Victorian England rested upon the underlying structure determined by social class.'[14] Class differences were a substantial factor of the Victorian society and unsurprisingly the grave differences between the classes led to different and distinctive views on ethics, work, domesticity and children in general. How much these views and perceptions differed will be pointed out in the following two sections.

---

[9] Tucker, Herbert: *A Companion to Victorian Literature and Culture*, p.70.
[10] Cf. Frost, Ginger: *Victorian Childhoods*, p.165.
[11] Kaplan, Fred: *Dickens – A Biography*, p.38.
[12] Kirby, Peter: *Child Labour in Britain, 1750-1870*, p.1.
[13] Kirby, Peter: *Child Labour in Britain, 1750-1870*, p.36.
[14] Mitchell, Sally: *Daily Life in Victorian England*, p.13.

2.1 The Middle-class – A romanticized Idealization

Speaking about the perception of children and childhood during the Victorian Era one usually refers to the ideas and ideals of the upper classes. It fact it was the Victorian middle-class that laid the foundation to the modern attitude towards childhood and which is closely intertwined with the perception of *the* ideal-typical and archetypical Victorian childhood as we imagine it today. It is not for nothing that 'family life […] was the most idealized part of childhood in the Victorian period'[15]. Especially the Romantic Movement's view on children as inherently innocent beings highly influenced Victorian middle-class parents' attitude towards their children and childhood in general[16]. The predominating image of the time in regard to children was definitely shaped by romanticized sentimentality: 'Children share certain important characteristics: they are depicted as infantile, with large heads or rosebud mouths or lips, and thus as innocent; as vulnerable, in need of adult protection; as trusting, perceiving only the good in the world.'[17]

But there was more to the middle-class view on children other that they were something immensely precious and worth protecting. As already mentioned above, class differences were a substantial part of society during the Victorian period and therefore shaped the views and opinions of those who were born into the different classes decisively. The foremost important aspect of the Victorian middle-class view on family life and childhood was the concept of domesticity: 'Domesticity was an idealization of the home. Home was a refuge from the cruelty and rapaciousness of the workplace and the marketplace.'[18] As a matter of fact, for the Victorian middle-class family the home had become especially important since it was seen as a tranquil haven within the vast and turbulent ocean of the hectic outside world. They tried to build their own little paradise of peace and serenity which stood in stark contrast to the public sphere. The Victorian middle-class tended to idealize the family and family life as a heavenly sanctuary with the luxury of leisure time, where loving mothers could play with their well-behaved children and fathers would relax after a long day of hard work. It is this 'new emphasis on the importance of the home [that] is a key element in Victorian Culture.'[19]

A direct connection to the concept of domesticity was the distribution of strict roles for all family members which was called the 'doctrine of separate spheres'[20]. Women were seen as

---

[15] Frost, Ginger: *Victorian Childhoods*, p.6.
[16] Cf. Frost, Ginger: *Victorian Childhoods*, p.143.
[17] Tucker, Herbert: *A Companion to Victorian Literature and Culture*, p.80.
[18] Steinbach, Susie: *Understanding the Victorians*, p.134.
[19] O'Gorman, Francis: *The Cambridge Companion to Victorian Culture*, p.220.
[20] Steinbach, Susie: *Understanding the Victorians*, p.134.

private creatures, the 'angels in the house' whose most important task was to care for the well-being of their children and husbands, even if that meant enormous personal sacrifices. They were expected to support their men in every way they could and while men made 'their living and their reputation in the world'[21], women were expected to be grateful towards their men, stay at home and 'tend the hearth and raise the children.'[22] Men on the other hand were public creatures and had to protect their beloved as well as to provide them with everything they needed. But not only the parents were bound to strict roles which they were ought to fulfill. They had precise expectations towards their children as well. Upper and middle-class children were supposed to be obedient, dutiful and grateful towards their parent's efforts and first and foremost should become respectable and honest adults in the future.[23] Education was an important factor in order to raise their children to become good adults. But since gender differences were especially strong within the upper and middle-classes, the different treatment of boys and girls concerning education started right from the beginning. Schooling was highly gendered in order to prepare the children for their respective gender roles for which they were destined as adults. Boys generally received more education, went to private or boarding schools and later on to universities whilst the girls stayed at their parent's house until they were decently married.[24] Oftentimes girls received less formal education, went to day schools or were educated by their mothers or a governess at home. In short, middle-class children usually grew up in a steady and protected environment and stayed 'children of the house'[25] until they could establish their own household – for girls this usually meant marriage while boys had to finish their schoolings and find a job first.

After looking at middle-class families and their attitude towards children and domesticity it becomes quite clear that only affluent people could afford such a lifestyle. Members of the wealthier classes 'had both the income and the leisure to pursue family lives as they pleased.'[26] The attitude of working-class parents towards their children and their overall living and working conditions showed a different and darker picture.

---

[21] Tosh, John: *A Man's Place – Masculinity and the Middle-Class Home in Victorian England*, p.1.
[22] Tosh, John: *A Man's Place – Masculinity and the Middle-Class Home in Victorian England*, p.1.
[23] Cf. Frost, Ginger: *Victorian Childhoods*, p.11.
[24] Cf. Frost, Ginger: *Victorian Childhoods*, p.28.
[25] Frost, Ginger: *Victorian Childhoods*, p.31.
[26] Frost, Ginger: *Victorian Childhoods*, p.21.

2.2 The Working-class – The economic Factor of Child Labour

In 1845 Politician Benjamin Disreale wrote about the different classes in England that the country was divided into two nations, the richer and the poor 'between whom there is no intercourse [...] as if they were dwellers in different zones.'[27] This contemporary citation shows the tremendous differences between the social classes in Victorian England. Due to the different circumstances of living which had almost nothing in common at all, the middle-class ideal of domesticity, the angel-like mother who cares for her demure, well-behaved children with a lot of leisure time and time to study simply couldn't be applied to working-class families. Stressed-out and drained working-class mothers were not uncommonly working full-time and on top of that had to handle the daily chores and make ends with the very little money the family had at its disposal. They simply had no time to play with their children or to educate them properly. Because of the parents' very restricted time and financial resources, working-class childhoods were decisively shorter than upper or middle-class ones. It was the need to start working at young ages that sharply divided the working-class from the middle-class.[28] Working-class children had to contribute to their family's financial situation as early as possible, mostly because of the father's low wages or for the many hungry mouths to feed. A children's 'non-work' and its long attendance at school or extensive leisure time were a luxury good a working-class family just couldn't afford.[29] The whole living environment of these children differed from that of their richer fellows: urban working-class families lived in unsanitary, overcrowded, cramped flats or row houses which were often notorious breeding grounds for diseases.[30] 'The cold, gray force of poverty'[31] and 'the narrowness of circumstances'[32] were the main reasons why children were sent to work as soon as possible. Whilst the middle-class home was a haven of peace and tranquility, the lodgings of the working-class remained places of work which provided little space and even less comfort. [33] Because of these reasons the distinctions in the length of childhood between the different classes were enormous. Although the legal age of majority in Britain at the time was twenty-one[34], a large number of working-class children went to work as young as seven, in some cases even younger.[35] As Jane Humphries puts it: 'Their most carefree years were those

---

[27] Steinbach, Susie: *Understanding the Victorians*, p.20.
[28] Cf. Frost, Ginger: *Victorian Childhoods*, p.74.
[29] Humphries, Jane: *Childhood and Child Labour in the British Industrial Revolution*, p.26.
[30] Cf. Frost, Ginger: *Victorian Childhoods*, p.13.
[31] Humphries, Jane: *Childhood and Child Labour in the British Industrial Revolution*, p.179.
[32] Humphries, Jane: *Childhood and Child Labour in the British Industrial Revolution*, p.179.
[33] Cf. Steinbach, Susie: *Understanding the Victorians*, p.21.
[34] Frost, Ginger: *Victorian Childhoods*, p.4.
[35] Frost, Ginger: *Victorian Childhoods*, p.4.

between the ages of two and three, from which they could walk and play, and about six, at which point they were expected to do chores and to care for younger siblings.'³⁶ Because poorer children had to support their family's financial position, they received decisively less education than their middle and upper-class peers and had to take more responsibilities at tender ages. Since schooling wasn't compulsory until 1870, the vast majority stopped schooling – if they ever had any at all – as soon as they could go to work. Schooling was expensive and most working-class parents couldn't raise the fees. Therefore, if they wanted their children to go to school, they had little choice about what type of school they could send their children to. Basically there were only two options left: many children went to Sunday Schools, which were free of charge and because classes were only on sundays, it didn't interfere with the child's work during the week. The second option formed the so-called Dame Schools, 'low-cost, ubiquitous institutions that took small, manageable groups of very young children and provided them with the basics.'³⁷ Dame Schools generally were less a place of education but rather a daycare for very young children while their parents were both out at work. The span of time a child could go to school and receive education crucially depended upon its parents' economic situation. This estimation becomes impressively apparent while looking at the 1851 census which stated that from the five million children between the age of three and fifteen living in Britain, only two million were actually attending *some sort* of school.³⁸ Gender differences also applied to the working-class. Girls received even less education than boys, they did more domestic chores than their brothers, worked for longer hours and less money.³⁹ Because most of the girls helped their mothers at home and/or cared for younger siblings, 'the attendance of girls at schools was consistently worse than that of boys.'⁴⁰ Another aspect which has to be taken into account while looking at the length of childhoods is the birth order of children. The oldest sibling usually had the shortest childhood because he had to take care of his younger siblings and went to work the earliest. Younger siblings often benefitted from their older siblings' earnings, meaning they could attend school for a longer time than their already working brothers and sisters. Children were often sent off to work in rank order.⁴¹

After taking a closer look at the perceptions of children and childhoods within the different social classes it can be said, that the children of the upper and middle-classes had decisively

---

[36] Humphries, Jane: *Childhood and Child Labour in the British Industrial Revolution*, p.143.
[37] Humphries, Jane: *Childhood and Child Labour in the British Industrial Revolution*, p. 371.
[38] Cf. Frost, Ginger: *Victorian Childhoods*, p.25.
[39] Cf. Frost, Ginger: *Victorian Childhoods*, p.31.
[40] Kirby, Peter: Child *Labour in Britain, 1750-1870*, p.118.
[41] Humphries, Jane: *Childhood and Child Labour in the British Industrial Revolution*, p.191.

longer childhoods than their peers form the working-classes, especially if one considers a children's own sentiment that its childhood ends as soon as it enters the world of employment and allegedly adulthood.[42] Most children saw the end of their childhood with the beginning of regular work outside the house.[43] It is a fact that 'even when child labour was wide spread, the children of the elite did not work'[44] just for the simple reason that economic considerations didn't force them to do so. For that reason alone the duration of childhood between the single classes was worlds apart. While working-class children went to work as early as possible to support their families with their income – at the beginning of Victoria's reign sometimes as early as only five years old – their affluent counterparts didn't go to work during their childhoods at all. Boys finished their schooling and academic training before they left home and started to work and girls were supposed to marry, not to work[45]. Working-class girls on the other hand were working as early and as much as their brothers, oftentimes even more. But upper and middle-class children hadn't had not only longer childhoods, they also stayed minors longer and were way more dependent on their parents' financial support than their working-class fellows. This resulted in the long lasting reliance of the affluent children on their parents, even though if they were already of legal age.[46] In addition to their longer childhoods it can also be said that better off children had fewer responsibilities, more and better education and therefore, better prospects in life. They had more hours of leisure but less freedom than their poorer peers who weren't always under the strict supervision of their parents.[47] Although working-class parents surely loved their children, they neither had the financial means nor the time to care for their children to that extend as upper and middle-class parents could.

They simply couldn't afford to offer their children an extended childhood. Poverty was the main reason why parents send their children to work at 'ages when their richer peers were deemed incapable of supporting themselves or of contributing to their family exchequer.'[48] In sum this means that a child's expectations largely depended 'on the economic status of the family and the child's sex, for both of these helped determine his or her future prospects.'[49]

---

[42] Cf. Kirby, Peter: *Child Labour in Britain – 1750-1870*, p.33.
[43] Cf. Frost, Ginger: *Victorian Childhoods*, p.74.
[44] Humphries, Jane: *Childhood and Child Labour in the British Industrial Revolution*, p.31.
[45] Cf. Frost, Ginger: *Victorian Childhoods*, p.31.
[46] Frost, Ginger: *Victorian Childhoods*, p.31.
[47] Cf. Humphries, Jane: *Childhood and Child Labour in the British Industrial Revolution*, p.143.
[48] Tucker, Herbert: *A Companion to Victorian Literature and Culture*, p.72.
[49] Frost, Ginger: *Victorian Childhoods*, p.11.

3. A Comment on Victorian Society - The Representation of Childhood and Child Labour in Charles Dickens' Novels

3.1 Oliver Twist

'Oliver Twist or the Parish Boy's Progress' is Charles Dickens' second novel and was first published in monthly instalments between February 1837 and April 1839 by the magazine 'Bentley's Miscellany'.[50] It is one of Dickens' best known and most influential works, having been adapted to several movie versions and theatre plays throughout the years and which hasn't forfeited any of its original charm until today. 'Oliver Twist' follows the life of the eponymous pauper orphan Oliver Twist who grows up in a workhouse where he and his companions are almost starving to death because of the stingy wardens. For a short time he gets apprenticed to an Undertaker but soon decides to run away from him because of ill-treatment. After wandering the streets of London he meets a boy nick-named the Artful Dodger, a young thief working for the devious Fagin who is the head of a whole gang consisting of child and teenage pick-pockets. Fagin and the boys show Oliver how to steal handkerchiefs and other valuable objects from pedestrians. Being caught in error by the police, Oliver almost gets arrested for stealing but luckily gets rescued by the generous and friendly Mr. Brownlow who takes him under his wings. After being abducted by Fagin's henchmen, the burglar Sikes and the prostitute Nancy, Oliver is forced to participate in a burglary and gets shot in the process but is nursed back to health by the friendly Mrs. and Miss Maylie who – after many trials and tribulations – help Oliver to find out more about his parents and where he actually comes from. After Fagin gets hanged because of his deeds Oliver can start a peaceful life in the countryside with his new friends.

What is extraordinary about 'Oliver Twist' is the very sarcastic narrator who oftentimes exposes the doings of single characters with the heavy use of irony and dark humour to ridicule. He mocks the hypocrisy of those who think they are doing beneficial things, although they are simply selfish and greedy egoists. Furthermore, Dickens delivers a very realistic portrayal of contemporary social injustices and cruelty against children as well as he gives very precise descriptions of the lives of society's outcasts like thieves and prostitutes. 'Oliver Twist' can very well be interpreted as a social satire which brought contemporary grievances like the waifs and strays of London, the terrible conditions of pauper children inside workhouses and the overall failures of the social system into the public eye. The following paragraphs will take a closer look at the depictions of the life of orphaned children

---

[50] Cf. Paroissien, David: *The Companion to Charles Dickens*, p.309.

inside workhouses, the custom of apprenticeship and child labour as well as the portrayal of the so called 'criminal-class' within Dickens' novel in order to understand his points of criticism.

3.1.1 Orphans and the Workhouse

Some of the probably most gloomy and depressive chapters of 'Oliver Twist' are those dealing with young Oliver's experiences inside the workhouse. Although, while reading these chapters they almost appear like an exaggerated caricature of actual events, Dickens does depict the sad truth of early Victorian England's attitude towards paupers in these chapters. The life of children inside workhouses under the New Poor Law of 1834 was especially harsh and unnecessary cruel. Workhouses were grim places to live in, especially since neither the Old, nor the New Poor Law was soft on children of the working-class and paupers.[51] In general it can be said that impoverished families on the verge of starvation saw workhouses as the dreaded 'last resort' they could go to, having only one choice left, as Charles Dickens accurately puts is: 'all poor should have the alternative […] of being starved by a gradual process in the house, or by a quick one out of it.'[52] This inhuman 'choice' exemplifies the great crux of the workhouses: Victorians tended to stigmatize poverty, paupers and everyone who had been in the workhouse since 'Victorian authorities feared that lessening the shame of pauperism or crime would result in increased laziness and violence.'[53] Many people of Dickens' time seriously believed that poverty was a direct result of moral degeneracy and that those who were poor deserved to suffer. In their eyes it was the paupers' own fault that they were poor because it was due to their 'inherent deficiencies'[54]. Therefore, the conditions inside the workhouse were kept bad and degrading on purpose because the life inside the workhouse should be even less appealing than the lowest paid job possible would be. It was thought that this would discourage 'lazy paupers' to come to the workhouse and rely on parish support simply because they were idle and work-shy.[55] Children who moved into the workhouse with their parents were rigidly separated from them and kept away from adults in general so they would not 'learn pauperism' from them and become adult paupers themselves.[56] The prevalent perception that living inside a workhouse should be humiliating and purposefully poor is mirrored in 'Oliver Twist' by The Board's completely distorted estimation on the living conditions inside a workhouse under the 'way too generous' Old Poor

---

[51] Frost, Ginger: *Victorian Childhoods*, p.45.
[52] Dickens, Charles, *Oliver Twist*, p.13.
[53] Frost, Ginger: *Victorian Childhoods*, p.9.
[54] Kirby, Peter: *Child Labour in Britain – 1750-1870*, p.95.
[55] Cf. Frost, Ginger: *Victorian Childhoods*, p.122.
[56] Cf. Frost, Ginger: *Victorian Childhoods*, p.123.

Law: 'the poor liked it! It was a regular place of public entertainment for the poorer classes; a tavern where there was nothing to pay; a public breakfast, dinner, tea and supper all the year round; a brick and mortar Elysium, there it was all play and not work.'[57]

Reality didn't look that bright. Especially for children, workhouses were particularly hard and an orphaned child without family or kin had the most disadvantages in life and the littlest prospects except from livelong stigmas.[58] How bad orphaned children fared is described in the following passage of 'Oliver Twist': Oliver was nothing but 'a parish child – the orphan of a workhouse, the humble, half-starved drudge – to be cuffed and buffeted through the world, despised by all, pitied by none.'[59] Although the children were kept on the edge of starvation on purpose, they should feel grateful for the charity they received, even if this charity barely prevented them from what would await them while living in the streets. That living inside the workhouse or in the streets didn't make that much a difference in regard to provision of food shows the following scene taken from Dickens' novel. The probably most famous scene of the entire book, the 'Please Sir, I want some more'-scene, where Oliver – after he 'and his companions [had] suffered the tortures of slow starvation for three months'[60] - dares to ask for a little more gruel and thereby starts an enormous uproar, illustrates the horrid conditions inside workhouses. And even though Dickens' surely does rely on artistic exaggerations when he makes the cook chase Oliver through the entire room and shows Mr. Bumble's and The Board's flabbergast reactions afterwards, the real life provisions of food inside workhouses were indeed minimal and unhealthy. One workhouse in Manchester for example had been reported to have fed its children entirely on a monotonous diet of nothing but oatmeal.[61] The poor food supply resulted directly in the usually poor health of the children raised inside workhouses. Oliver, who is described as 'a pale, thin child, somewhat diminutive in statue, and decidedly small in circumference'[62] is no exception.

---

[57] Dickens, Charles: *Oliver Twist*, p.13.
[58] Cf. Frost, Ginger: *Victorian Childhoods*, p.121.
[59] Dickens, Charles: *Oliver Twist*, p.4.
[60] Dickens, Charles: *Oliver Twist*, p.15.
[61] Cruickshank, Marjorie: *Children and Industry - Child health and welfare in North-West textile towns during the nineteenth century*, p.37.
[62] Dickens, Charles: *Oliver Twist*, p.6.

3.1.2 Apprenticeship and Child Labour

Although these aspects are only mentioned on the sidelines of 'Oliver Twist', apprenticeships and child labour both occur throughout the novel and without question the scene were Oliver just barely escapes the fate of being employed by the brutal master sweep Mr. Gamfield is one of the first really frightening and thrilling moments of the novel.

Apprenticeships have always been common in English history, way before the rise of the Industrial Revolution – actually the importance of apprenticeships was slowly but surely on decline during the Victorian Age[63]. Nonetheless, there was the 'wide spread belief in its value'[64] which leads to the estimation that apprenticeship still was an important factor that determined the further lives and future prospects of children decisively during the time when Charles Dickens wrote 'Oliver Twist'. An apprenticeship was a formal agreement between a child and a master who was supposed to introduce his apprentice to his trade. Masters usually paid a premium (ranging from 2 to 10 pounds) to secure the service of a child.[65] Many parents voluntarily sent their children to masters who would teach them a respectable trade in order to enable them a better future with regular earnings. In this context it was also reported that parents paid fees to the masters.[66] Generally spoken, an apprenticeship was a formal contract between the master and the parents of the children he was supposed to train. Therefore, the masters were obliged to several duties: they 'provided him [the apprentice] with board and lodging, introduced him to the modus operandi of his trade and safeguarded his moral welfare'[67] as well as they showed the children the 'mysteries' of the trade. The reverse of the medal formed those children who were without such a formal agreement between their parents and a master, which was usually the case with orphans and pauper children. First of all, there was a distinct difference between the types of trades to which pauper children and private apprentices were bound to since pauper children had little to no choice in regard to their futures[68]. As Ginger Frost puts it: 'the state chose where they lived, where they went to school and when and where they were employed'.[69] Many pauper children were sent to work as early as seven and suffered under cruel or drunken masters who were simply in search of cheap labour.[70]

---

[63] Humphries, Jane: Childhood and Child Labour in the British Industrial Revolution, p.258.
[64] Cf. Humphries, Jane: Childhood and Child Labour in the British Industrial Revolution, p.263.
[65] Cf. Paroissien, David: The Companion to Oliver Twist, p.79.
[66] Cf. Frost, Ginger: Victorian Childhoods, p.59.
[67] Humphries, Jane: Childhood and Child Labour in the British Industrial Revolution, p.263.
[68] Cf. Kirby, Peter: *Child Labour in Britain – 1750-1870*, p.38.
[69] Frost, Ginger: *Victorian Childhoods*, p.140.
[70] Cf. Frost, Ginger: *Victorian Childhoods*, p.58.

The reader of 'Oliver Twist' finds the practice of 'selling' young pauper children to dubious masters in order to get 'rid of destitute children'[71] in form of the obviously sadistic and cruel master sweep Mr. Gamfield. The New Poor Law policy after 1834 thought that pauper children, who lived inside workhouses and thus relied entirely on parish support, were supposed to contribute to their subsistence. In order to get them off the poor rates, many children were bound to the very first master who would be willing to pay the fee for their services. This is exactly what happens to Oliver who is barely ten years old when he is supposed to be apprenticed: 'orphaned, deserted or illegitimate children in parish care usually found themselves apprenticed at very early ages.'[72]

Just like in Oliver's case when 'the public was once more informed that Oliver Twist was To Let, and that five pounds would be paid to anybody who would take possession of him'[73] there could in fact be found advertisements of orphaned children from the workhouse in local newspapers of the time.[74] Vulnerable children were sold to the highest bidder – for Oliver Twist this almost meant Mr. Gamfield who represents the one trade to which pauper children were often brokered to: chimney sweeps apprentices. The master sweep Mr. Gamfield is purposefully depicted as a brutal man, he bestows blows upon the head of his donkey and 'did happen to labour under the slight imputation of having bruised three or four boys to death already'[75] which qualifies him in the eyes of the parish beadle Mr. Bumble as exactly 'the sort of master Oliver Twist wanted'[76]. What reads like a sky high exaggeration of actual events can indeed be underpinned with real life accounts. Of course this does not refer to all master sweeps, but there were for sure many master sweeps notorious for been overly brutal to their apprentices.[77] George Elson, a former chimney sweeps apprentice wrote in his biography: 'the master spent most of the money the boys earned from them to riotous drinking, consequently their wretched apprentices were brutally kicked and beaten if they failed to obtain such by some means fair or foul.'[78] Angus Wilson calls Mr. Gamfield's behaviour in front of the magistrate a 'callous mix of sadism and ingratiation.'[79] He is someone who can only inflict pain on others because of the connivance of The Board, those who were responsible for the well-being of the workhouse children. Although Oliver manages by a hair's breadth to escape being apprenticed to Mr. Gamfield, the reader still gets a pretty clear

---

[71] Paroissien, David: *The Companion to Oliver Twist*, p.79.
[72] Kirby, Peter: *Child Labour in Britain – 1750-1870*, p.38.
[73] Dickens, Charles: *Oliver Twist*, p.27.
[74] Cruickshank, Marjorie: *Children and Industry*, p.13.
[75] Dickens, Charles: *Oliver Twist*, p.21.
[76] Dickens, Charles: *Oliver Twist*, p.19.
[77] Cf. Frost, Ginger: *Victorian Childhoods*, p.68.
[78] Frost, Ginger: *Victorian Childhoods*, p.68.
[79] Wilson, Angus: *The World of Charles Dickens*, p.310.

idea of how a life as a chimney sweeps apprentice would have been like for him. Even if 'Oliver Twist' does not focus on child labour in general, there are still some scenes in which it gets mentioned. One stands in direct connection to Mr. Gamfield and Oliver's supposed apprenticeship. One member of the magistrate calls it 'a nasty trade'[80] and another states that 'young boys have been smothered in chimneys before'[81] when he refers to chimney sweeps apprentices. Exemplarily for the employment of very young children in extremely dangerous environments this section will take a closer look at the so called 'climbing boys'. At the time when Charles Dickens wrote 'Oliver Twist' the Chimney Sweepers Act of 1834 had just raised the minimum age at which children were allowed to be employed as chimney sweeps apprentice to ten.[82] Formerly children even as young as six were sent up flues.[83] The work was hard and extremely dangerous for several reasons. The boys were climbing up the chimneys and cleaning them by hand from dust and soot which meant they were inhaling fine dust, sulphur and soot particles all the time.[84] This permanent inhalation of toxic substances led to the occupational disease called Chimney Sweeps Cancer or 'soot wart' at which will be taken a closer look under section 4.2 of this work. In general the principle and most common cause of death for climbing boys was suffocation, due to their passing through soot in very narrow flues.[85] Some children burnt to death in ablaze chimneys whose fires they were supposed to extinguish. Because the children had to climb up the chimneys in the way a caterpillar would do while were wearing little to no clothing in the process, injuries were frequent, elbows and knees that were supporting the whole weight of the child were scraped raw[86]. Some of the flues were as narrow as nine square inch, heavily implying the danger of being jammed and stuck in the chimneys.[87]

In addition to the already dangerous environment and working conditions, many master sweeps were – as already mentioned above – outright cruel. One practice of the master sweeps was particularly dangerous for the children and it is exactly this practice Mr. Gamfield refers to in front of the magistrate. In order to make the children work faster, some master sweeps lighted a small fire of straw or a brimstone candle in the fireplace – it should

---

[80] Dickens, Charles: *Oliver Twist*, p.20.
[81] Dickens, Charles: *Oliver Twist*, p.20.
[82] Cf. Paroissien, David: *The Companion to Oliver Twist*, p.65.
[83] Cf. Strange, K.H.: *Climbing Boys. A study of Sweeps' Apprentices, 1773-1875*, p.4.
[84] Cf. Frost, Ginger: *Victorian Childhoods*, p.68.
[85] Cf. Strange, K.H.: *Climbing Boys. A study of Sweeps' Apprentices, 1773-1875*, p.67.
[86] Cf. Strange, K.H.: *Climbing Boys. A study of Sweeps' Apprentices, 1773-1875*, p.30.
[87] Cf. Frost, Ginger: *Victorian Childhoods*, p.68.

encourage the child to climb faster.[88] When one of magistrate's members says that some boys have been suffocated in the process Mr. Gamfield replies in a self-confident manner:

'That's acause they damped the straw afore they lit it in the chimbley to make 'em come down agin […] That's all smoke, and no blaze; vereas smoke ain't o' no use at all in making a boy come down, for it only sinds him to sleep, and that's wot he likes. Boys is wery obstinit, and wery lazy, gen'lmen, and there's nothing like a good hot blaze to make 'em come down vith a run. It's humane too, gen'lmen, acause, even if they've stuck in the chimbley, roasting their feet makes 'em struggle to hextricate theirselves.'[89]

What eventually rescues Oliver from the fate of being a little climbing boy is the new law of 1834 which stated that children who were supposed to become chimney sweeps apprentices had to express in front of a magistrate that they were 'willing and desirous'[90] to be apprenticed to this particular trade. Oliver makes it very clear that he is anything but willing and desirous when he falls on his knees and 'prayed that they would order him back to the dark room – that they would starve him – beat him – kill him if they pleased – rather than send him away with this dreadful man.'[91] It was Oliver's chance that being apprenticed by a chimney sweep required the child's consent. Other workhouse children who were employed by dubious masters in trades they didn't like weren't that lucky. David Paroissien even argues that the children's forceful employments to jobs they neither wanted nor liked, bound to masters or employers who were complete strangers, harsh and sometimes even brutal, led many of those apprentices who were formerly in the parish care into a life of crime.[92] Because these children were not bound to family ties and loyalty, they were searching for an alternative to the harsh conditions of work. The seemingly lucrativeness of thieving formed such an alternative, a point which will directly lead over to another important aspect of children's lives in Victorian society portrayed by Charles Dickens: thieves and prostitutes.

---

[88] Cf. Strange, K.H.: *Climbing Boys. A study of Sweeps' Apprentices, 1773-1875*, p.26.
[89] Dickens, Charles: *Oliver Twist*, p.20.
[90] Strange, K.H.: *Climbing Boys. A study of Sweeps' Apprentices, 1773-1875*, p.31.
[91] Dickens, Charles: *Oliver Twist*, p.26.
[92] Cf. Paroissien, David: *The Companion to Oliver Twist*, p.2.

3.1.3 Thieves and Prostitutes

The contemporary concern about juvenile crime was high during the early part of the Victorian period, even resulting in an increasing fear of it. This newly arising concern might have resulted from the broad visibility of stray children inhabiting the streets of St. Giles, Seven Dials, Saffron Hills, Whitechapel and Spitalfields. There were swarms of street children that 'congregated in the cities, begging and thieving to survive'.[93] Stray children were visible everywhere and 'everyone walking through a large city saw vagrant, dirty children, begging on the streets or sleeping in parks.'[94] The omnipresent child poverty brought this social problem into public focus - for the year of 1840 it was estimated that some 10.000 children were scratching a living in the streets of London alone. For many orphaned, abandoned or impoverished children, thieving and begging oftentimes were the only alternative to a life in the dreaded and highly stigmatized workhouse whose terrible conditions have already been explained earlier. It isn't a surprise that many juvenile offenders commented rather positively on the relative lucrativeness of thieving in contrast to the wretched life inside workhouses or the exploitative work in factories and workshops.[95] Parental neglect, lack of education, family disruption and debilitating environments were all possible culprits which caused children to start a life of delinquency[96] but above all, poverty was a 'root cause'[97] for most youth's crimes. Especially the capital was closely associated as being a breeding ground for juvenile offenders: 'London played a central role in the conceptualization of juvenile crime; a close association was made in the minds of contemporaries between the social problems of the metropolis and the rise of the juvenile crime.'[98] The so classed 'criminal-classes' and the idea of the 'the criminal underworld' were both closely entwined with the contemporary perception of London.[99] Having that in mind it is not surprising that Dickens chose London of all places to be the setting for most of his novels darker chapters.

When nowadays readers think about juvenile and child criminality in Victorian England - especially in London - the image of the Artful Dodger and Charley Bates will almost inevitably come to their minds. Boys, not older than maybe twelve or thirteen, are already skilled and shrewd pick-pockets with the attitude and style of grown men. What concerned

---

[93] Frost, Ginger: *Victorian Childhoods*, p.146.
[94] Frost, Ginger: *Victorian Childhoods*, p.104.
[95] Cf. Shore, Heater: *Artful Dodgers – Youth and crime in early nineteenth century London*, p.39.
[96] Shore, Heather: *Artful Dodgers – Youth and crime in early nineteenth century London*, p.22.
[97] Frost, Ginger: *Victorian Childhoods*, p.140.
[98] Shore, Heather: *Artful Dodgers – Youth and crime in early nineteenth century London*, p.149.
[99] Shore, Heather: *Artful Dodgers – Youth and crime in early nineteenth century London*, p.149.

the contemporary commentators on juvenile criminals the most was that these children frequently developed the mannerism of adults and so it was very hard to decipher their actual stage of maturity and whether they were able to take responsibility for their actions or not.[100] This phenomenon of children who behaved like little gentlemen can also be discovered in 'Oliver Twist' in the form of the Artful Dodger and his companions: 'Seated round the table were four or five boys, none older than the Dodger, smoking long clay pipes, and drinking spirits with the air of middle-aged men.'[101] Although these are still young boys, Dickens heavily implies that they - and especially the Artful Dodger - are in the 'trade' for a long time and hence very cunning and experienced. The description of Jack Dawkins, also known as the Artful Dodger – whose nickname already gives a broad hint towards his talents – simply doesn't fit the description of a boy his age: 'He had about him all the airs and manners of a man. His hat was stuck on top of his head, […] he wore a man's coat which reached nearly to his heels. […] He was, altogether, a roystering and swaggering a young gentleman as ever stood four feet six, or something less, in his bluchers.'[102] It can be said that Dickens shows the reader with his character the epitome of the young, but already experienced and allegedly worldly-wise pick-pocket. It is exactly this juxtaposition between real age and experience that posed a great problem to the courts of the time: 'Clear it was felt that tender age not automatically correlated to innocence and inexperience'.[103] In the same year when the first chapter of 'Oliver Twist' was published, over 2000 children between the age of seven – the age which was generally supposed as the time when a child was able to distinguish between right and wrong – and sixteen went to jail.[104] This high number was the direct result of the fact that neither law nor courts made a real distinction in the way they treated child and adult defendants.[105] Children up from the age of seven were convicted to the same punishments as grown men, meaning that children as young as nine years were sentenced to a transportation to the colonies.[106] Transportation to the colonies was an integral part of juvenile punishment and especially often applied to young male defendants.[107] It's the very same fate that befell the Artful Dodger who, after he had been arrested for stealing a gentlemen's snuff box, gets sentenced to what Fagin calls 'lagging and lifer'[108]: transportation for life. Even though this sentence appears rather harsh for today's standards, Ginger Frost argues that certain crimes

---

[100] Cf. Shore, Heather: *Artful Dodgers – Youth and crime in early nineteenth century London*, p.3.
[101] Dickens, Charles: *Oliver Twist*, p.71.
[102] Dickens, Charles: *Oliver Twist*, p.66.
[103] Shore, Heather: *Artful Dodgers – Youth and crime in early nineteenth century London*, p.9.
[104] Frost, Ginger: *Victorian Childhoods*, p.132.
[105] Cf. Frost, Ginger: *Victorian Childhoods*, p.132.
[106] Cf. Frost, Ginger: *Victorian Childhoods*, p.133.
[107] Cf. Frost, Ginger: *Victorian Childhoods*, p.132.
[108] Dickens, Charles: *Oliver Twist*, p.40.

tended to attract more often a sentence of transportation than others, simply because the offenders of such crimes were perceived as being more experienced criminals. Those accused of pick-pocketing, the very crime the Artful Dodger is charged with, were very prone to receive a sentence of livelong transportation. Therefore, it can be said that Dickens' descriptions of the lives of the young delinquents and their subsequent sentences indeed picture the reality and zeitgeist of the time.

Closely connected to the worries about thieves and pick-pockets were the contemporary attitude towards prostitution. Prostitution and prostitutes were seen as an enormous social problem; the belief that it was shattering and endangering the moral framework of the Victorian society was strong throughout all social classes. The often quite young girls (most of the thousands of prostitutes in London were between 15 and 22 years of age[109]) who were working as prostitutes in the streets of the slums and seedy quarters of greater cities were considered even worse and morally tainted than pick-pockets and robbers. Just like juvenile criminality and child labour in general – although a very extreme example, prostitution of young girls can be counted under the label of child labour as well - the two principal factors which were forcing young girls to work in the streets were extreme poverty and parental abandonment.[110] Their devastating economic situation and lack of alternatives pushed many girls into street prostitution. How many there were exactly, is illustrated by the 1841 London census which calculated the city's population 'as 2,103,279, making a ratio of approximately four prostitutes to every one hundred individuals.'[111] Dickens' character of the teenage-girl Nancy is one of them. Even though it is never outright mentioned throughout the novel that Nancy works as a prostitute, her initial description when she enters Fagin's den and meets Oliver for the first time, left little to no doubt to the Victorian readership that she and her friend Beth were working the streets indeed: 'They wore a great deal of hair, not very neatly turned up behind, and were rather untidy about the shoes and stockings. They were not exactly pretty, perhaps; but they had a great deal of colour in their faces, and looked quite stout and hearty. Being remarkably free and agreeable in their manners, Oliver thought them very nice girls indeed. And there is no doubt they were.'[112]

Especially the mentioning of their 'remarkably free and agreeable manners' in combination with their dressed up appearance and loads of make-up in their faces made their 'profession' obviously clear to the reader. It is not surprising that Dickens chose to show prostitutes in his

---

[109] Cf. Cody, David: *Child Labour*
[110] Paroissien, David: *The Companion to Oliver Twist*, p.238.
[111] Paroissien, David: *The Companion to Oliver Twist*, p.17.
[112] Dickens, Charles: *Oliver Twist*, p.78.

novel as well when he made the decision to show thieves and dens. Girls often lived with young thieves and were employed by experienced criminals for whom they worked, just like Nancy had worked for Fagin for many years – first as a pick-.pocket and later on as a prostitute. Sometimes the girls even seduced young boys into a life of crime.[113] The girls supported themselves and thereby maintained the boys and the elder criminal figure by their prostitution and by occasional stealing from the men they had picked up in the streets.[114] Regardless of the fact that all these aspects are never actually shown in 'Oliver Twist' either, it is very likely that the Victorian readership who was enormously concerned about juvenile criminals and the 'great social evil'[115] of prostitution, was aware of at least some of these points.

Further important aspects in regard to the description of Nancy - except from her noble act of helping Oliver which will be discussed later - are her relationship with Sikes and her interaction with the hotel staff she meets, when she wants to speak to Rose Maylie. Nancy's dysfunctional relationship with Sikes is shaped by massive violence as well as physical and psychological abuses. It is left open by Dickens whether Sikes is Nancy's pimp but it is very likely that he is. When Paroissien describes that prostitutes tended to attach themselves to a single man and even after 'ill-treatment, blows, wounds and even broken limbs are not capable of shaking their attachment to some men'[116], this behavior can be transferred one-to-one to Nancy. Notwithstanding that Sikes threatens and maltreats her, she states that she is 'drawn back to him through every suffering and ill-usage'.[117] This is probably the most shocking part for the Victorian readership about Nancy's behaviour. Her refusal to leave Sikes can be seen as a perversion of the middle-class ideal regarding the morals of a faithful and loving woman. Nancy is utterly and downright faithful and loyal towards Sikes until the very end. She rigorously refuses to leave him, even though she has several chances to do so and leave her old life behind, e.g. when Mr. Brownlow and Rose Maylie offer her a life in an asylum. This devotion and absolute faithfulness towards a man, even under enormous personal sacrifices, were the foremost attributes associated with a well-behaved middle-class woman who should support her husband under any circumstances and no matter what. It is

---

[113] Cf. Paroissien, David: *The Companion to Oliver Twist*, p.108.
[114] Cf. Paroissien, David: *The Companion to Oliver Twist*, p.110.
[115] Paroissien, David: *The Companion to Oliver Twist*, p.4.
[116] Paroissien, David: *The Companion to Oliver Twist*, p.239.
[117] Dickens, Charles: *Oliver Twist*, p.374.

this irrevocable loyalty to a man what Nancy describes as 'the one feeling of a woman left'[118] in her, even though this feeling only leads into 'new means of violence and suffering'.[119]

The second aspect of great importance in connection to Nancy's work as a prostitute is the tangible disdain for these girls, which becomes especially apparent in the scene where Nancy wants to speak to Rose Maylie for the first time in a hotel. Because of her appearance that obviously denounces her as a harlot, the hotel staff doesn't even want to let her see Rose Maylie: 'you don't suppose the young Lady will see such as her, do you?'[120] Nancy is looked down upon by the staff members - especially by the female staff-members - with 'virtuous disdain'[121] and called 'a creature [that is] a disgrace to her sex'.[122] It is even advocated by two maids that Nancy should be 'thrown ruthlessly into the kennel'.[123] Such reactions mirror the overall scornful attitude of the Victorian society – throughout all social classes – towards prostitutes. The girls were perceived as completely adulterated and lost 'beyond all hope of redemption'[124] because of the sexual nature of their transgression. Dickens puts the general attitude and prevailing opinion of his contemporaries towards prostitutes into this very scene but simultaneously tries so raise compassion and sympathy for the girl who desperately tries to do something good. Statements like 'I am the infamous creature […] that lives among the thieves, and that never from the first moment I can recollect my eyes and senses opening on London streets have known any better life, or kinder words than they have given me'[125] intend to explain the circumstances and living conditions which have forced girls like Nancy and so many others into a life of delinquency and misery. Dickens' tries to arise pity for this poor girl who knew only the harsh life in the streets of London's slums right from the cradle.

---

[118] Dickens, Charles: *Oliver Twist*, p.376.
[119] Dickens, Charles: *Oliver Twist*, p.376.
[120] Dickens, Charles: *Oliver Twist*, p.368.
[121] Dickens, Charles: *Oliver Twist*, p.368.
[122] Dickens, Charles: *Oliver Twist*, p.368.
[123] Dickens, Charles: *Oliver Twist*, p.368.
[124] Shore, Heather: *Artful Dodgers – Youth and Crime in early nineteenth century London*, p.10.
[125] Dickens, Charles: *Oliver Twist*, p.371.

3.2 David Copperfield

'David Copperfield' or 'The Personal History Experience and Observation of David Copperfield the Younger of Blunderstone Rookery' is Charles Dickens' eighth novel and was as well as its predecessor 'Oliver Twist' published in monthly instalments between May 1849 and November 1850 by Bradbury and Evans.[126] 'David Copperfield' is a Bildungsroman which focusses on the personal development of the young middle-class boy David Copperfield throughout his childhood and teenage years. It is the personal history of a boy who tries to find his place in the world. Written in first-person perspective David writes and comments on his own biography in the retrospective when he is already a famous author. The novel covers several important stages in a child's and later on teenager's life like being sent to a boarding school, making friends and falling in love, finding suitable employment as well as dealing with the death of beloved ones. With certainty it can be said the 'David Copperfield' is one of Dickens' most autobiographic novels and was clearly one of his personal favourites as this comment on his work shows: 'Of all my books, I like this the best. It will be easily believed that I am a fond parent to every child of my fancy, and that no one can ever love that family as dearly as I love them. But, like many fond parents, I have in my heart of hearts a favourite child. And his name is David Copperfield.'[127]

Taking the novel's status as its creator's favourite into account, it is not surprising that 'David Copperfield' – although its main focus lays on a middle-class boy – contains several aspects of social criticism on topics which were important to Dickens. The reader witnesses with anguish the powerlessness of children. He experiences how David's evil stepfather beats and misuses him, sends him to a boarding school where the maltreatment continues and right after his mother dies, his stepfather forcefully employs David to work at a bottling factory where the young boy suffers greatly.

In addition to the content of the novel the style of writing also deserves closer attention. Although the narrator of the story is already a gown up man, the chapters in which he is very young are described and seen through the innocent and naïve eyes of a child. The language does evolve together with the main protagonist. Dickens' shows the thoughts, emotions and beliefs of a child in a very empathic and credible way and thus gives the reader explicit insight into his main character and his sentiments. It is not for nothing that 'David Copperfield' is still one of the most famous novels dealing with the repression of children

---

[126] Cf. Paroissien, David: *The Companion to Charles Dickens*, p.368.
[127] Dickens, Charles: *David Copperfield – Introduction by Carabine, Keith*, p.12.

even today. In fact Dickens was 'one of the first writers to pay close attention to child characters in his works.'[128]

But even though 'David Copperfield' does contain a lot of social criticism, it mainly focusses on the middle-class and therefore many aspects do not fit into the conception of this paper. Due to that the following part of the work will focus primarily on the chapters in which David is forced to work at the bottling factory of Murdstone and Grinby, his developing friendship with the hopelessly debt-ridden Mister Micawber and the treatment of the fallen working-class girl little Em'ly. The analysis of these chapters will be in regard to the aspects of child labour, the working and overall living conditions of the working-class, as well as Dickens' criticism on those topics in connection to his own biography.

3.2.1 Child Labour in Factories

How much Dickens' own experiences as a child influenced the writing of 'David Copperfield' becomes most apparent in the chapters which are dealing with David's enforced employment at the bottling factory of Murdstone and Grinby. While writing these chapters Dickens drew heavily on his own childhood experiences[129] when he was a twelve-year old boy and already employed at Warren's Blackening Factory, a factory producing shoe-polish in a warehouse by the side of the Thames.[130] It can be said with certainty that Charles Dickens to great lengths wrote about his own biographic experiences as a child when he was writing the scenes which are taking place at Murdstone and Grinby in 'David Copperfield'. David Paroissien even goes so far as calling Dickens' childhood experiences at the blackening factory outright 'traumatic'[131] and exactly this traumatic feeling does Dickens deliver to the readership of his novel.

Right after the death of his mother, David - at the time only ten years old – stops going to school and becomes 'a little laboring hind in the service of Murdstone and Grinby.'[132] Although not a working-class boy himself, he shares the fate of many working-class children who were employed at factories and workshops because of their families strained financial situation. These children were not uncommonly employed at even more tender ages as ten. The work at the bottling factory which David has to perform is rather monotonous and repetitive. He has to wash and label bottles of wine, bottle corks and put seals upon the corks.

---

[128] Dickens, Charles: *David Copperfield – Introduction by Carabine, Keith*, p.10.
[129] Cf. Sutherland, John: *The Longman Companion to Victorian Fiction*, p.172.
[130] Mee, Jon: *The Cambridge Introduction to Charles Dickens*, p.2.
[131] Paroissien, David: *The Companion to Charles Dickens*, p.316.
[132] Dickens, Charles: David Copperfield, p.135.

The work isn't heavy and in no regard such hard manual work as it could be found in other industrial branches, but there are other aspects to his work which make the time in the factory a living hell for David. What Dickens excellently points out in these chapters is the degradation of those children working at factories. Like David they were successively stripped off any friendly attention, counsel and emotional support and felt completely left on their own during their working-shifts.[133] This feeling of loneliness and abandonment is the main reason why after a few weeks of work at Murdstone and Grinby a ten year old boy comes to the devastating conclusion that he is 'utterly without hope now.'[134] It is this degradation and exploitation of vulnerable children that Dickens prominently features in these chapters and which are the most horrible aspects of working at the factory for David as well. He doesn't even mind the work itself as much as he is concerned about the feeling of being utterly and totally left alone in this cold and anonymous world full of strangers and people he doesn't like. He is left without a single soul to turn to. Because of this particular feeling of utter isolation he turns into a 'lonely child'[135] and if one considers his age when he starts to work at Murdstone and Grinby, it is only natural that such a young boy would feel totally abandoned and been sold down the river: 'I suffered in secret, and that I suffered exquisitely, no one ever knew but I. How much I suffered, it is […] utterly beyond my power to tell.'[136] The sentiments of David are an example that can very well be applied to other children in similar situations since 'what differed in the industrial age, then, was not the fact of work but its character. Factory jobs meant a long day of almost constant toil, paced by steam-driven machines, under the supervision of strangers in unhealthy conditions.'[137] And even though the working conditions could have been a lot worse for David, if one thinks about the terrible conditions inside cotton mills for example, the conditions under which David has to work are certainly unhealthy and dangerous for a child. His descriptions of the warehouse where the factory is located in are anything but reassuring. He calls the warehouse 'a crazy old house with a wharf of its own […] and literally overrun with rats. Its panelled rooms, discoloured with the dirt and smoke of hundred years […] decaying floors and staircases; the squeaking and scuffling of old grey rats down the cellars; and the dirt and rottenness of the place.'[138] The impression the reader gets while reading those lines is that of a terrible place to live and work in. It is a sad fact that during the time when Dickens wrote 'David Copperfield' the main

---

[133] Cf. Wilson, Angus: *The World of Charles Dickens*, p.317.
[134] Dickens, Charles: *David Copperfield*, p.136.
[135] Angus, Wilson: *The World of Charles Dickens*, p.216.
[136] Dickens, Charles: *David Copperfield*, p.142.
[137] Frost, Ginger: *Victorian Childhoods*, p.44.
[138] Dickens, Charles: *David Copperfield*, p.134.

problem with smaller factories and workshops were the terrible building conditions[139] – quite often the buildings were nothing more but decaying huts, infested by rats and other vermin and without any fresh air supply. The real life conditions inside the factory where Charles Dickens' had to work as a child read exactly like his descriptions of the warehouse of Murdstone and Grinby: A 'crazy, tumble-down house… on the river… literally overrun with rats.'[140] But most of the time children had no choice where they had to work. Like in David's case, the children's parents usually decided where their offspring went to work. For many families of Dickens' time children's labour was necessary because of the low wages of most unskilled workers.[141] As a matter of fact children were most likely to be working at young ages if the head of the household was an unskilled worker or if the family was headed by a lone parent.[142] Child labour wasn't an invention of the industrialized times but it gradually changed over the centuries. For decades many children had been working in the agricultural sector or were employed in domestic service, especially popular for girls. Both sectors had been places of work for children long before the Industrial Revolution but as Ginger Frost has already stated above, working in factories was something completely new and a direct result of the industrialization. Work took the children out of their homes. Half of the day they were away from their families, kin and friends and put under the control of adults who were complete strangers.[143] Working in factories meant long hours of work for poor wages. David's meagre salary is no exception, his payment for one week of monotonous labour amounts to only six shillings[144], the average wage for a boy his age. Boys were earning an average of seven shillings, girls just five.[145] Dickens' own payment at Warren's Blackening Factory had been six shilling as well.[146] The even lower payment of children in contrast to the already low wages of adult workers and the urging need of many working-class families - the so called 'labouring poor'[147] - to support their financial situation with additional income were the main reasons why child labour became so attractive for employers. Factory and workshop owners employed children because 'they were cheap, did not complain, had nimble fingers

---

[139] Cf. Frost, Ginger: *Victorian Childhoods*, p.59.
[140] Kaplan, Fred: *Dickens. A Biography*, p.38.
[141] Frost, Ginger: *Victorian Childhoods*, p.55.
[142] Kirby, Peter: *Child Labour in Britain – 1750-1870*, p.28.
[143] Cruickshank, Marjorie: *Children and Industry - Child health and welfare in North-west textile towns during the nineteenth century*, p.3.
[144] Dickens, Charles: *David Copperfield*, p.137.
[145] Cruickshank, Marjorie: *Children and Industry - Child health and welfare in North-west textile towns during the nineteenth century*, p.61.
[146] Cf. Kaplan, Fred: *Dickens. A Biography*, p.38.
[147] Cruickshank, Marjorie: *Children and Industry - Child health and welfare in North-west textile towns during the nineteenth century*, p.6.

and could crawl under machines.'[148] Or as Marjorie Cruickshank puts it: 'With their sharp eyes, nimble fingers and small, agile bodies children were considered indispensable to the factory regime.'[149] Oftentimes children were cheaper to use for the factory owners than to invest into

the few machines available for the repetitive tasks children like David had to fulfill.[150] And although Dickens himself wasn't one of 'the urban poor or one of those thousands of economic migrants increasingly drawn to the city, the experience nevertheless seems to have given him a sharp sense of the uncertainty of life for those in the lower classes of the vibrant but harsh metropolis.'[151] It's exactly this understanding for the life of working-class people that becomes apparent while reading 'David Copperfield'.

3.2.2 Debtor's Prison

In direct connection to David's employment at Murdstone and Grinby stands his acquaintance and subsequent friendly attachment to his poor landlord Mr. Micawber and his family. David quickly befriends the family and is overly happy to finally have some friends he can turn to. Unfortunately, the happiness doesn't last long due to Mr. Micawber's constant financial problems which finally result in his arrestment at debtor's prison. Mr. Micawber and his family are portrayed as friendly and simple people but their finances are a complete disaster: 'I have known him come home to supper with a flood of tears, and a declaration that nothing was now left but jail'.[152] The strained financial situation depresses and affects the whole family until 'Mr. Micawber's difficulties came to a crisis, and he was arrested early one morning, and carried over to the King's Bench Prison in the Borough.'[153] After almost the whole household equipment and furniture of the Micawber's is sold away, Mrs. Micawber resolves to take her children and move into the prison as well. The family is finally set free again after Mr. Micawber applies for his release under the Insolvent Debtors Act, a decision dreaded by most debtors since it demanded that the possessions of a family should not be valued at more than twenty pounds.[154] The episode of Mr. Micawber's imprisonment can also be directly related to Charles Dickens own biographic experiences as a child. Due to his debts, Charles Dickens' father John Dickens got arrested in February 1824 because of his

---

[148] Cody, David: *Child Labour*
[149] Cruickshank, Marjorie: *Children and Industry - Child health and welfare in North-west textile towns during the nineteenth century*, p.146.
[150] Cf. Kaplan, Fred: *Dickens. A Biography*, p.38.
[151] Mee, Jon: *The Cambridge Introduction to Charles Dickens*, p.2.
[152] Dickens, Charles: *David Copperfield*, p.143.
[153] Dickens, Charles: *David Copperfield*, p.145.
[154] Cf. Kaplan, Fred: *Dickens. A Biography*, p.39.

incapability to repay fourty pounds. He was imprisoned just two weeks after Charles had started to work at the blackening factory.[155] John Dickens was quickly moved to the Marshalsea Prison and soon afterwards his whole family - except for Charles who was supporting his family with his earnings from his employment and was living at friends of the family during the time - followed him there.[156] Imprisonment for debts quickly affected whole families: most of the family's possessions were pawned or sold in order to repay the debts and get the father out of prison. In John Dickens' case it is only after he had declared himself an 'insolvent debtor' that he was released from prison per Insolvent Debtors Act in May 1824.[157] The fate of the Micawber family stands exemplarily for many families who were forced to follow the imprisoned father into prison since the main problem with sending insolvent debtor's to prison was that their imprisonment simultaneously affected their wives and children as well. Because the man usually was the main, sometimes even the only earner, whole families where deprived of a regular income. This can be seen as the main reason why many wives of debtor's prison inmates decided to move into the prison and take their children with them, as Mrs. Micawber and Mrs. Dickens decided to do, because they could not maintain a life outside. Sending debtors and subsequently their whole families to prison was quite counterproductive for the repayment of the debts. Since fathers couldn't work at the time they were imprisoned and thus couldn't earn money, the financial problems which brought the family into prison in the first place prevailed. The only option to get out of prison apart from repaying the money was to apply to the court and declare oneself an insolvent debtor via the Insolvent Debtor's Act whose negative consequences have already been explained above. Dickens' own thoughts upon the matter might shine through in the form of Mr. Micawber who, while still in prison, 'composed a petition to the House of Commons, praying for an alteration in the law of imprisonment for debt. [158]

3.2.3 Fallen Women

The image of the fallen and seduced woman was a common theme in Victorian literature and art. Since women in general were seen as morally superior to men and were sometimes even seen as the moral guardians of society, the transgression of fallen women was especially grave and vehemently condemned by contemporary commentators. Thus it is not surprising to find this particular theme several times among the many others 'David Copperfield' provides. Most prominently it can be found in form of the story of little Em'ly. Little Em'ly's life hasn't

---

[155] Cf. Mee, Jon: The Cambridge Introduction to Charles Dickens, p.2.
[156] Kaplan, Fred: *Dickens. A Biography,* p.39.
[157] Cf. Kaplan, Fred: *Dickens. A Biography*, p.39.
[158] Dickens, Charles: *David Copperfield*, p.147.

been especially joyful when she meets David Copperfield for the first time while he visits Peggotty's relatives in Yarmouth. Em'ly is the orphaned child of a fisherman who died at sea and subsequently got adopted by her uncle, the brother of David's nursemaid Peggotty. She is a childhood friend of David and his first 'love'. But right at the beginning of the novel, when the reader starts to develop an attachment to Em'ly, Dickens makes very clear that a grim future will await the little girl when he lets David ponder at the beach while watching her balancing on a piece of wood above the sea: 'Would it have been better for little Em'ly to have had the waters close above her head this morning in my sight? And when I have answered, Yes, it would have been.'[159] This grim prediction of the girls prospects results from her dissatisfaction of her current situation. Even as a little girl Em'ly expresses unhappiness about her social status. She rather wants to be a lady instead of a fisherman's wife when she grows up. When she would accomplish to become a lady she could have 'a sky-blue coat with diamond buttons, nankeen, trousers, a red velvet waistcoat, a cocked hat, a large golden watch, a silver pipe, and a box of money'[160] to give to her uncle and she and her family could be 'gentlefolks together'.[161] This wish for a better life and social advancement makes her vulnerable and receptive for false promises and subsequently is the main cause for her fall into disgrace. She leaves her fiancé, her cousin Ham who loves her dearly, in favour of the rich but terribly tainted character of David's school friend James Steerforth. Steerforth is a shady, two-faced character who befriends David at boarding school. Being a member of the upper-class he is spoiled, rich and used to get what he desires. Seduced by the hope of a life as a lady Em'ly gets herself into a relationship with Steerforth who not even in the slightest intends to marry the girl and soon gets tired of her company after their elopement. After the sad realization that she has eloped for absolutely nothing, Em'ly flees the villa in Naples where she had stayed with Steerforth but is too ashamed and frightened to return back home. It is only due to her uncles desperate and constant searching and the help of the former prostitute Martha that she can finally be tracked down in London. The description of the place where Martha finally finds Em'ly is especially worrying since it is heavily implied that it might be a brothel: 'The house swarmed with inmates. As we went up, doors of rooms were opened and people's heads put out; and we passed other people on the stairs […] It was a broad panelled staircase, with massive balustrades of some dark wood; cornices above the doors, ornamented with carved fruits and flowers; and broad seats in the windows. But all these tokens of past grandeur were miserably decayed and dirty […] Two or three times, by the way, I thought I observed in the indistinct light the skirts of a female between us and the

---

[159] Dickens, Charles: *David Copperfield*, p.36.
[160] Dickens, Charles: *David Copperfield*, p.34.
[161] Dickens, Charles: *David Copperfield*, p.35.

roof.'[162] After she is found by her uncle she decides to emigrate to Australia to start a new life in the colony. Although fallen women were despised by the Victorian society, Dickens does try to raise some pity for Em'ly when he lets her explain her view on the matter during the discussion with Miss Dartle, an upper-class woman who had also cast an eye on Steerforth. Em'ly does very well understand the gravity of her elopement and what the consequences of her doings are and consequently is terribly ashamed of herself. Throughout the novel Em'ly is depicted as a nice but naïve and simple girl who only knows the good-hearted, honest simplicity of her family and kin. It didn't come to her mind that Steerforth saw nothing else in her but a nice diversion. Dickens does not justify Em'ly's doings but he still implies that the affluent son of landed-gentry was the one who deceived her and therefore is the one to blame for the young girls fall and eventual seduction. Dickens delivers reasons for her transgression and gives her the chance to explain her motives for it during her confrontation with the furious Miss Dartle who embodies all resentments of the Victorian society against unfaithful woman. During that scene Em'ly only retorts to her disdainful accusations: 'I had been brought up as virtuous as you or any lady [...] If you live in his home and know him, you know, perhaps, what his power with a weak, vain girl might be. [...] That he used all his powers to deceive me, and that I believed him, trusted him, and loved him!'[163] Dickens lets the despised and deceived girl explain her reasons and views on the matter and by doing that he gives the fallen woman a voice to defend herself against the brought forth accusations. His compassion for the girl might become most apparent in the ending Dickens chose for Em'ly.

Though he portrays without any whitewashing the devastating and enormously consequences of Em'ly's behavior for herself and especially for her family, he still gives the unhappy, deceived girl a moderately happy ending by letting her emigrate to Australia where she can recover a normal life and start anew, something which wouldn't have been possible in Victorian society.

---

[162] Dickens, Charles: *David Copperfield* p.609.
[163] Dickens, Charles: *David Copperfield* p.612.

3.3 Dickens' Criticism of social Injustices

Oliver Twist

After looking at both novels and their descriptions of poor children and wretched childhoods, two question arise: What were Dickens' aims in writing about pauper children, abusive parents, neglectful guardians, workhouses and the hard work of children in factories since these were all topics his Victorian readership didn't particularly want to read about? Dickens himself stated 'that some might find both his subject matter and his social critique offensive', so what might have been his reasons to write about these topics in the way he did and most importantly, what does his choice say about his personal views on the matter? To answer the last question first it can be said that his opinion about workhouses, the treatment of the poor and orphaned children in addition to the general failures of the British social system after the New Poor Law of 1834 become particularly obvious while reading 'Oliver Twist'. 'Oliver Twist' is a social satire[164] with a lot of direct and indirect criticism as mentioned above. The author uses heavy irony and a narrator who decidedly takes sides for the poor and helpless while revealing in his sarcastic comments on the character's actions the cruelty of those who think they are doing charitable things but are in fact only worsening the already bad circumstances, like Mr. Bumble, Mrs. Mann or Mrs. Corney.[165] Dickens' portrayal of the failures of the charity system and public policy towards the poor as well as the outright horrible treatment and stigmatization they received by society are put in a nutshell by Angus Wilson who states: 'Oliver Twist [...] is a story of the routine cruelty exercised upon the nameless, almost faceless submerged of Victorian society by a system, which would be harsh if efficient, given the built-in inefficiency of human beings, is deadly'.[166] By exposing this inefficiency to the general public, Dickens heavily tackles his contemporary's views on paupers as lazy and work-shy people and purposefully depicts the workhouse as what it really was: the last resort poor people would turn to[167] because they had only two choices left: 'Being starved by a gradual process in the house or by a quick one out if it.'[168] Both the New Poor Law of 1834 and the workhouse were in Dickens' eyes lacking humanity and it was this very humanity he was appealing to in his critique.[169] Dickens' Victorian readership was very likely to held views that only marginally differed from those of Mr. Bumble, the Board or Mrs. Corney. There was the wide spread idea that paupers should be grateful to be in the

---

[164] Cf. Wilson, Angus: *The World of Charles Dickens*, p.129.
[165] Cf. Wilson, Angus: *The World of Charles Dickens*, p.129.
[166] Wilson, Angus: *The World of Charles Dickens*, p.129.
[167] Frost, Ginger: *Victorian Childhoods*, p.124.
[168] Dickens, Charles: *Oliver Twist*, p.13.
[169] Cf. Paroissien, David: *The Companion to Charles Dickens*, p.164.

workhouse and if they would go to work, there wouldn't be a need for them to live inside the workhouse in the first place. What Dickens achieves by describing the workhouse and its inmates in the way he does is the realization that it usually weren't the so called 'able-bodied' paupers who had to find refuge in workhouses. What Dickens is describing in his novel are the old, the very young and the ill, exactly those three groups who made up the great majority of workhouse inmates in reality: 'in 1859 only 16 percent of those in poor law institutions were able-bodies adults, 42 percent were non-able-bodied adults, and 38 percent were children.'[170] His contemporaries who argued in favour of the workhouse didn't take into account the terrible conditions under which many paupers had to live both outside and inside these institutions. 'Early Victorian society was a cruel jungle – most cruel to the plain poor, who could fall no lower'.[171] This point Dickens tries to criticize throughout the first chapters of 'Oliver Twist' which are dealing with Oliver's experiences inside the workhouse – for Dickens 'all the institutions of Oliver's society constitute a 'systematic course of inhumanity''[172] and were an 'icon of social injustice'.[173] Therefore, he uses the 'victimization of the workhouse orphans as a fictional attack on contemporary attitudes and abuses, thus initiating a novel of serious social concern'[174]. Another very prevalent aspect of criticism which becomes apparent throughout the novel refers to the Victorian perception that poor children were seen as inherently evil and as soon as they were born already tainted by their bad environment. The view that Oliver is nothing but a little, ungrateful troublemaker and that nothing good could ever be expected from him gets very clear in the way Mr. Bumble and the Board's member who's wearing the white waistcoat react towards him. Although Oliver did nothing wrong apart from asking on the edge of starvation for a little more gruel and is purposefully depicted as inherently *good and innocent,* they see and treat him as someone who does nothing but mischief, even leading to the estimation of the Board's member 'that the boy will be hung.'[175] The poor, illegitimate orphaned boy Oliver is deliberately depicted as an angelic character who can't even fathom evilness or malice. Oliver seems to be resistant to the Victorian idea that 'circumstance bends and distorts human nature.'[176] This contradiction can be seen as a challenge to the Victorian assumption that paupers and criminals were already tainted and evil at birth and that the children of the very poor were

---

[170] Paroissien, David: *The Companion to Charles Dickens*, p.164.
[171] Wilson, Angus: *The World of Charles Dickens*, p.48.
[172] Paroissien, David: *The Companion to Charles Dickens*, p.309.
[173] Paroissien, David: *The Companion to Charles Dickens*, p.308.
[174] Paroissien, David: *The Companion to Charles Dickens*, p.308.
[175] Dickens, Charles: *Oliver Twist*, p.16.
[176] Mee, Jon: *The Cambridge Introduction to Charles Dickens*, p.22.

naturally corrupted as products of a hardened environment that 'cradled [them] in iniquity'.[177] Oliver couldn't possibly have grown up under worse circumstances yet he is beyond any doubt absolutely and inherently good-natured. What Dickens tried to show his middle-class readers with this almost unbelievably good boy is that an evil environment does not necessarily taint a human being. Dickens' opinion about what happens if the environment changes a human being for the worse can be seen in the form of Dickens' other famous orphaned character the Artful Dodger. His character can be understood as the epitome of 'crime was the result of the terrible poverty and ignorance in Victorian society'[178] and that an environment which became corrupted by the terrible living conditions was most likely the main reason for malice and crime, not inherent vice. Despite the fact that the Artful Dodger is indeed a shady character with many flaws, he still does care about his friends and is anything but inherently evil or depraved. After taking a closer look at them it can be said that the depiction of both orphaned boys serves a certain purpose. Throughout his writing career Dickens 'worked hard on society's compassion in order to diminish the poverty and the ignorance'[179] and in the case of 'Oliver Twist' he achieves this goal by making an ill-treated, little boy his main character for whom even the most steel-hearted person would have to feel sympathy and pity for. Although Charles Dickens himself stated that he feared 'that there are in the world some insensible and callous natures, that do become utterly and incurably bad'[180] (like for example Fagin) he tries to show two things with the characters of his novel: as above mentioned he tries to demonstrate with the character of Oliver that the environment does not necessarily turn a human being into a criminal. Oliver stays good-hearted, innocent and faithful until the end, although he experiences in his short life almost nothing but cruelty, grief, loneliness and abandonment. In regard to Oliver's superhuman goodness, Jon Mee even goes as far as calling children Dickens' 'items of morality'[181]. In fact it can be argued that the character of Oliver works as a vehicle to deliver 'an image of humanity worked upon by curl, which exploits poverty and ignorance'[182]. On the other hand Dickens tries to show that even people who the society saw as absolutely 'past all hope'[183] and lost beyond redemption are capable of noble, compassionate acts. This is most impressively done by the character of Nancy. As a prostitute and therefore thought of by the Victorian society as abysmally adulterated, she commits the most compassionate act in the entire novel when she sacrifices

---

[177] Cf. Shore, Heather: *Artful Dodgers – Youth and crime in early nineteenth century London*, p.35.
[178] Wilson, Angus: *The World of Charles Dickens*, p.131.
[179] Wilson, Angus: *The World of Charles Dickens*, p.131.
[180] Wilson, Angus: *The World of Charles Dickens*, p.131.
[181] Mee, Jon: *Cambridge Introduction to Charles Dickens*, p.35.
[182] Wilson, Angus: *The World of Charles Dickens*, p.131.
[183] Dickens, Charles: *Oliver Twist*, p.434.

her own life in order to help Oliver, thus leading to the interesting fact that 'Nancy's compassion erodes the previously clear-cut distinction between villains and victims.'[184] It also erodes the perception of Dickens' contemporary readership. The Victorian society thought it impossible that such a tainted person like a prostitute would be able of doing such a noble act. The presentation of Nancy as a person doing good shows a sympathetic consideration of prostitutes which was 'far in advance of Dickens' contemporaries in their comments on this great social evil.'[185] Dickens' explanation why Nancy has become corrupted can be interpreted as an overall approach to call upon the society's humanity. He wants to arise pity, sympathy and above all understanding for that poor girl whose 'life had been squandered in the streets, and among the most noisome of the stews and dens of London'[186] but who has nonetheless 'something of a woman's original nature still left in her'[187]. But he does not only appeal towards the reader's sentiments, he makes it also quite clear that it is to a great extent the fault of society – due to the above mentioned ignorance and inhumanity – that women like Nancy had to live the lives they were living: 'Oh dear lady, why ar'n't those who claim to be God's own folks as gentle and as kind to us poor wretches as you, who, having youth, and beauty, and all that they have lost […]?'[188] Dickens couldn't have made his point more clear as when he lets Nancy resume his criticism upon society in one simple sentence: 'If there was more like you, there would be fewer like me.'[189]

David Copperfield

In the second novel 'David Copperfield' the social critique is a lot more subdued than it is in its predecessor 'Oliver Twist'. Dickens' social critique oftentimes isn't obvious at first glance. Since 'David Copperfield' isn't a social satire but more a coming-of-age story or Bildungsroman[190], it deals to great lengths with typical adolescence problems every young person has to deal with at some point in life. For example it can be mentioned the wish to find true friends and the associated process of understanding that not every person who pretends to be your friend is really friendly. The novel covers topics like children and young adults going to school and studying in order to find a suitable profession, falling in love with all the good and bad consequences of infatuations and the overall aim to find one's place in life. It is the

---

[184] Paroissien, David: *The Companion to Charles Dickens*, p.314.
[185] Paroissien, David: *The Companion to Oliver Twist*, p.4.
[186] Dickens, Charles: *Oliver Twist*, p.369.
[187] Dickens, Charles: *Oliver Twist*, p.369.
[188] Dickens, Charles: *Oliver Twist,* p.430.
[189] Dickens, Charles: *Oliver Twist*, p.371.
[190] Wilson, Angus: *The World of Charles Dickens*, p.215.

story of a middle-class boy who learns his lessons in life[191] and that depicts the 'troubled quest for identity'[192].

But nonetheless, Dickens does utter his views on contemporary grievances. This is most impressively done during the episode where David is forced to work at the bottling factory of Murdstone and Grinby. The probably most interesting fact about his critique during these chapters is that Dickens does not condemn or tackle child labour in general but focusses more on the conditions under which children had to work and which negative consequences these conditions might have had for them. While reading those pages it really is astonishing that David is definitely most concerned about his social status and not about the work itself. He was born into a middle-class family and feared that his employment at a factory and the companionship of 'lower class and ignorant'[193] comrades might cause him to fall from class.[194] It is interesting indeed that 'David does not mind the work so much as the degrading company it forces him to keep'[195]. The awareness of classes and social belonging was very strong in Charles Dickens himself, and probably because of this profuse class-consciousness, Dickens does offer criticism about sending children to work in 'David Copperfield'. He impressively describes the sentiment of a child that feels like it had been totally abandoned while living all on its own at such a tender age. This description gives an insight to what might result from the feeling of being completely alone and neglected in an unknown environment. Charles Dickens himself stated that after having been sent to work at the blackening factory he was nothing but 'a small boy, ill-lodged, underfed, often aimlessly wandering the streets.'[196] David Copperfield goes even further when he says that he could have easily turned 'from the care that was taken from me, [into] a little robber or a little vagabond.'[197] Like Charles Dickens, Copperfield aimlessly wanders the street, works in bad companionship, earns little - only six shilling and week[198] - and has even less to eat. David feels completely stripped off any love, affection and attention: 'No advice, no counsel, no encouragement, no consolation, no support of any kind, from any one, that I can call to mind, as I hope to go to heaven.'[199] Though Dickens doesn't criticize as directly and openly as he did in 'Oliver Twist', the reader of these chapters sees and understands the transformation of David quite well – the reader experiences at first-hand how working in a factory could change

---

[191] Wilson, Angus: *The World of Charles Dickens*, p.215.
[192] Peck, John: *David Copperfield and Hard Times*, p.2.
[193] Kaplan, Fred: *Dickens. A Biography*, p.39.
[194] Paroissien, David: *The Companion to Charles Dickens*, p.316.
[195] Peck, John: David Copperfield and Hard Times, p.35.
[196] Wilson, Angus: *The World of Charles Dickens*, p.58.
[197] Paroissien, David: *The Companion to Charles Dickens*, p.316.
[198] Dickens, Charles: *David Copperfield*, p.137.
[199] Dickens, Charles: *David Copperfield*, p.140.

a child to the worse and sees how David 'turns into a shabby child'[200] that feels completely left alone and vulnerable. In addition to that Dickens also names and shames the repetitive work and the consequences which such work had on the feelings and psyche of children that were employed at such factories. The similarities between Dickens' descriptions of his own work at the blackening factory and what the reader gets while reading 'David Copperfield' are strikingly obvious. David says about his work at Murdstone and Grinby: 'When the empty bottles ran short, there were labels to be pasted on full ones, or corks to be fitted to them, or seals to be put upon the corks, or finished bottles to be packed in cask.'[201] It almost sounds exactly like what Dickens said about his own employment at Warrant's Blackening Factory when he spent his days covering 'pots of paste-blacking, first with a piece of oil-paper, and then with a piece of blue paper'[202] and was repetitively plastering labels onto pots of black shoe polish. Throughout the pages which are dealing with the factory it becomes exceptionally apparent that a bad environment, the monotonous work and the feeling of being totally left alone in the entire world were the reasons which led to the devastating estimation of David that puts Dickens views on this topic into a nutshell. A young boy who has his full life ahead of him states that he felt 'utterly without hope'[203] when 'the secret agony of his soul, […] his early hopes of growing up to be a learned and distinguished man, crushed in his breast.'[204]

Furthermore, it can be added that Dickens did show sympathy for the so-called fallen women of society like little Em'ly in his novel. He doesn't clearly take up position against the disdainful treatment of those women, but the fashion in which he is writing about Em'ly reveals a certain amount of compassion and understanding for her situation instead of just plain condemnation. He heavily implies that it isn't always the woman who's to blame when he lets Em'ly explain her reasons for the elopement with Steerforth. He gives the fallen woman a voice and the possibility to explain and defend herself against the society's accusations brought forth in the form of Miss Dartle. In a very discreet and subtle way Dickens' triggers a very important emotion in his reader: sympathy. He achieves to raise sympathy and understanding for a girl that has loved once but lost everything: her good reputation, her former lifestyle and her home.

---

[200] Dickens, Charles: *David Copperfield*, p.146.
[201] Dickens, Charles: *David Copperfield*, p.135.
[202] Paroissien, David: *The Companion to Charles Dickens*, p.316.
[203] Paroissien, David: *The Companion to Charles Dickens*, p.316.
[204] Kaplan, Fred: *Dickens. A Biography*, p.39.

In conclusion it can be said that Charles Dickens' fictional works were full of social criticism and denouncement of society. It can even be said that he acted as 'a denunciator of social evils'[205] when he choose to write about the prevailing contemporary problems of the time by unveiling and condemning injustices like persecutions, cruelty and the oppression of the weak and poor.

---

[205] Low, Sampson: *Giants of Literature – Charles Dickens*, p. 35.

4. Health and Safety-concerns

4.1 Accidents and Dangers at Work

Working places in the early Victorian Age could be extremely dangerous grounds for adults and children alike. Due to unsecured, heavy machinery like power looms and steam engines as well as to the humid and heavily polluted air inside the factories, the working conditions were quite often hard, unhealthy and perilous. To young children, small and therefore likely to be overlooked, playful and inattentive, this environment posed even greater threats as it was the case for their parents. There were several reports on 'toddlers, who were overrun in the streets, […] young chimney sweeps who had suffocated in flues and, above all, factory children were killed by machinery or by steam boilers explosions.'[206]

Work related accidents involving children were frequent. Factories and cotton mills in particular posed several serious dangers for their young employees. A moment of distraction, childish carelessness, fatigue or general exhaustion were the main reasons why many children lost fingers or whole limbs after they got caught and dragged into the moving machinery parts.[207] Accidents appeared en masse mainly at the end of shifts when children were especially tired and drained by the long hours of standing at their work places.[208] Until the Factories Act of 1844 twelve-hour-shifts were common even for children, 'steam-driven machinery set the pace of work'[209] which forced children 'to stay awake and alert beyond their natural capacities.'[210] Cases were recorded were children fell asleep and got killed in an accident.[211] Girls were particularly endangered by accidents since their long hair and loose, flying garments were prone to be drawn into the revolving shafts of the machines.[212] In regard to that Marjorie Cruickshank argues that 'accidents were often due to unguarded movements in the slippery aisles between machines. They were also the result of children being set to clean machinery while it was still in motion.'[213] The cleaning of working machinery was particularly common in cotton mills. Since children were small enough to crawl under the

---

[206] Cruickshank, Marjorie: *Children and Industry - Child health and welfare in North-west textile towns during the nineteenth century*, p.7.
[207] Cf. Cruickshank, Marjorie: *Children and Industry - Child health and welfare in North-west textile towns during the nineteenth century*, p.97.
[208] Cf. Cruickshank, Marjorie: *Children and Industry - Child health and welfare in North-west textile towns during the nineteenth century*, p.42.
[209] Frost, Ginger: *Victorian Childhoods*, p.65.
[210] Frost, Ginger: *Victorian Childhoods*, p.65.
[211] Cf. Frost, Ginger: *Victorian Childhoods*, p.67.
[212] Cf. Cruickshank, Marjorie: *Children and Industry - Child health and welfare in North-west textile towns during the nineteenth century*, p.42.
[213] Cruickshank, Marjorie: *Children and Industry - Child health and welfare in North-west textile towns during the nineteenth century*, p.51.

weaving looms and mend broken threads or clean the machine's components without interrupting the workflow, this practice proved to be especially harmful. Another factor contributing to the comparatively high rate of accidents in factories in comparison to other sectors where children found employment was the habit of paying factory workers at piece rates. The harder and especially faster the children worked, the more money they received at the end of the day, putting the children under extreme pressure and tempting them to work hastily and to make hectic movements.[214] In addition to these already bad circumstances came the overall unhealthiness of most factories which - due to machines becoming heated and the reliance on coal and steam engines for power supply - tended to be hot and humid places without little to no access to fresh air, making the work especially hard and exhausting.

4.2 Work related Diseases and long term Effects on Life Expectancy

In addition to the harsh environment many children had to live and work in, as well as to the accidents that regularly occurred while operating heavy machinery, the working conditions of the children often were outright hazardous. The following section will deal exemplarily with two typical, entirely work related diseases which primarily endangered children.

Deformities of the Bones

The outer appearance of children who had started to work at factories or workshops at very young ages differed considerably from those of their non-working peers. Due to standing for - in the worst cases - up to twelve hours a day during a time when their bones were not completely developed, deformities of the bones and physical deprivations were a common result. Factory children were especially prone to curved spines, crooked or twisted limbs and unsightly joints. Even contemporary medical investigators reported 'significant defects of the physique of urban factory children compared to rural children'[215] as well as they stressed on the negative long term effects in regard to the physical and mental development of the children. Factory work starting from early ages changed the appearance of children to the worse as the following citation illustrates: 'the most startling contrast with our own day would undoubtedly be their physical appearance. We would notice the smaller statue and pinched faces, particularly of working children, the unsightly joints and crooked limbs, the scars and open sores, the number of cripples in irons and clutches and, above all, the prevalence of dirt

---

[214] Cf. Cruickshank, Marjorie: *Children and Industry - Child health and welfare in North-west textile towns during the nineteenth century*, p.49.
[215] Cruickshank, Marjorie: *Children and Industry - Child health and welfare in North-West textile towns during the nineteenth century*, p.94.

and discomfort in flea-bitten bodies and infested hair.'[216] A second common reason for bone deformities was Rickety, an illness caused by vitamin deficiency which was already associated with malnutrition and general bad living conditions at the time.[217] Among other things Rickety caused the limbs of the children to bend and crook which was the reason why these children were colloquially referred to as 'factory cripples'[218], a term which puts the negative effects of heavy manual labour for long hours on young children to the point.

Chimney-sweep's Cancer (Soot wart)

The term chimney-sweep's cancer (commonly called 'soot wart') refers to an occupational disease caused by working in an unhealthy environment which caused a carcinoma of the skin of the scrotum due to inhaling soot and a 'large quantity of charcoal, sulphur, and ammonia'[219] over a long period of time. Chimney-sweep's cancer was the first disease where surgeons recognized the working conditions of the patients as the main source of danger, making it the first recorded occupational cancer in history. This sort of cancer in particular affected mostly teenagers and young adults because of the large amount of children working as chimney sweeps apprentices (an estimation of the 1830's assumed there were 5 million children in Britain apprenticed to that particular trade[220]). The so called climbing boys had to go up the chimneys and clean them by hand. While crawling up the narrow flues, they inhaled a lot of dust, soot and grime in the process. This constant contact with these substances gradually damaged the respiratory passages and the lungs of the boys. As climbing boys (and sometimes girls) were often very young when they started (so they would easily fit into the narrow flues they had to clean), grown up climbing boys often had been in contact with soot since their early childhood.[221] After the longstanding negative affection of their lungs and airways from a tender age, the cancer manifested quite early, usually during their late teens or early twenties, shortening their life expectancy dramatically. Few former climbing boys lived to the age of fifty, most of them died considerably younger.[222]

---

[216] Cruickshank, Marjorie: *Children and Industry - Child health and welfare in North-West textile towns during the nineteenth century*, p.2.
[217] Cf. Cruickshank, Marjorie: *Children and Industry - Child health and welfare in North-west textile towns during the nineteenth century*, p.41.
[218] Cruickshank, Marjorie: *Children and Industry - Child health and welfare in North-west textile towns during the nineteenth century*, p.41.
[219] Paroissien, David: *The Companion to Oliver Twist*, p.66.
[220] Paroissien, David: *The Companion to Oliver Twist*, p.66.
[221] Cf. Strange, K. H.: *Climbing Boys. A study of Sweeps' Apprentices, 1773-1875*, p.65.
[222] Paroissien, David: *The Companion to Oliver Twist*, p.66.

5. Contemporary Perception of Child Labour

The views and opinions regarding the benefits and dangers of child labour were anything but consistent in Victorian society. Views differed greatly in regard to social classes, ethics and moral views as well as in terms of economic considerations. Due to the financial contribution of their offspring, many working-class families were dependent on their children going to work and heavily relied on their earnings - whether the parents or children liked that fact or not. By sending their children to work as soon as possible, in many cases the provision of a higher living standard for the entire family could be achieved.[223] Due to the pressing financial situations, many working-class families had no real choice in the matter. Athough 'Many middle-class reformers […] blamed the boy's parents, […] economic necessity was a much more likely culprit.'[224] But even throughout the middle and upper-classes the views on working children varied greatly. There were voices who argued in favour of child labour, as well as there were others who were determinedly against the employment of children (one famous example would be Lord Shaftesbury). A strong argument in favour of employing children mentioned by its middle-class supporters was the idea that children of the working-class had to be occupied in order to keep them off the streets. There was the strong belief that poor, unattended children would gradually glide into a life of deprivation and crime if they wouldn't do something beneficial for society since their 'youthful spirits must be curbed early.'[225] Employing children in a trade or in a factory was seen as a convenient and easy way of 'turning the restless energy of childhood into productive channels.'[226] The many street urchins, the so call 'street-arabs' and pickpockets who were inhabiting the poorer districts of greater cities gave further support to that theory. Many contemporaries were utterly shocked by the so called 'vagrant children' – street children (or sometimes only children playing in the streets, because their parents were off to work) with way too much independence.[227] The street was seen as a place of corruption and contagion for young, easily influenced people.[228] Because of that 'the typical middle-class view […] was, that it was impossible to imagine a more healthy and reasonable mode of bringing up a child than in occupying it in some practical and useful work for one half of the day and engaging him in study for the other

---

[223] Cf. Kirby, Peter: *Child Labour in Britain 1750-1870*, p.5.
[224] Frost, Ginger: *Victorian Childhoods*, p.64.
[225] Cruickshank, Marjorie: *Children and Industry - Child health and welfare in North-West textile towns during the nineteenth century*, p.2.
[226] Cruickshank, Marjorie: *Children and Industry - Child health and welfare in North-West textile towns during the nineteenth century*, p.2.
[227] Cf. Kirby, Peter: *Child Labour in Britain, 1750-1870*, p.70.
[228] Cf. Shore, Heather: *Artful Dodgers – Youth and crime in early nineteenth-century London*, p.24.

half.'[229] Although this view does include the wish for education for working-class and pauper children it also reveals some serious double standards in regard to the opinion of the middle-class, since their own children didn't work until they had either finished their studies or were married. Furthermore, it was thought that this charitable idea of preventing children from a life in the streets and keeping them into the straight and narrow had the positive side-effect that there would be less criminals and pauper adults in the care of the state later: 'If children were to be prevented from falling into mischief and crime – and later into a life of indigence and depravity that would make them a burden on society – they must be subdued and accustomed to habits of industry.'[230] Many contemporaries thought it was simply the right thing to employ the children of the poor in order to keep them out of mischief. Hand in hand with this fear of the wealthier classes that poor children might indulge into a life of crime goes the conviction that the factories were healthier than the often extremely dirty and confined accommodations in which the children lived in. It was believed that 'in contrast to the public and domestic squalor the factory was clean, dry and spacious and afforded 'a moderate degree of healthy exercise''.[231] Many middle-class supporters of child labour in factories seemed to have a completely wrong idea about the working conditions in mills, factories or in coal mining. In fact, many factories, especially those with a great heat generation like for example cotton mills, were a breeding ground for infectious diseases due to the concentration of many people in hot, humid rooms with little to no ventilation.[232] In contrast to these assertions that child labour was something good for the children and something even better and beneficial for society do stand the arguments of the opponents of child labour. Most vociferously in form of the above mentioned Lord Shaftesbury who publicly uttered his opinion that working children were unfree labourers whose lives differed hardly from those of slaves.[233] Other opponents of child labour argued likewise 'that factory children were overworked, stunted and prematurely aged'.[234] Because of the rising dissident with the practice of child labour there were several attempts by the government to counter the employment of children - or very young children at least - and their exploitation and abuse. As one indication for the rising recognition of this social problem can be seen the legislations passed for the purpose of protecting children at

---

[229] Cruickshank, Marjorie: *Children and Industry - Child health and welfare in North-West textile towns during the nineteenth century*, p.96.
[230] Cruickshank, Marjorie: *Children and Industry - Child health and welfare in North-West textile towns during the nineteenth century*, p.2.
[231] Cruickshank, Marjorie: *Children and Industry - Child health and welfare in North-West textile towns during the nineteenth century*, p.53.
[232] Cf. Cruickshank, Marjorie: *Children and Industry - Child health and welfare in North-West textile towns during the nineteenth century*, p.20.
[233] Cf. Kirby, Peter: *Child Labour in Britain - 1750-1870*, p.97.
[234] Frost, Ginger: *Victorian Childhoods*, p.66.

work. Philanthropists and humanitarians like Lord Shaftesbury condemned child labour on moral grounds since they feared the decline of the integrity of the family as well as moral degeneracy. Hence they tried to promote the middle and upper-class ideal of family life in order to prevent parents from sending their children off to work at an early age.[235] Unfortunately, they didn't take into account that in many working-class households the middle-class ideal of an angel-like mother doing nothing but nurture her children simply wasn't applicable due to the mother's own occupation, as already explained in this work's 2nd section. For many working-class parents sending their children to work meant a necessary evil. The well-meaning middle and upper-class philanthropists who tried to save the children didn't think about that fact that 'factory children were able to make a significant contribution to family income.'[236] Because of that Kirby argues that: 'The enactment of laws to regulate the employment of children almost always had a depressive effect upon the income of poor families but child labour laws never contained provisions to compensate parents for the loss of their children's earnings.'[237] The report of a 1861 commissioner in Newcastle goes in line with this argumentation: 'If the wages of a child's labour are necessary, either to keep the parents from the poor rates, or to relieve the pressure of a severe and bitter poverty, it is far better that it should go to work at the earliest stage at which it can bear the physical exertion than that it should remain at school.'[238]

---

[235] Cf. Kirby, Peter: *Child Labour in Britain – 1750-1870*, p.94.
[236] Cruickshank, Marjorie: *Children and Industry - Child health and welfare in North-west textile towns during the nineteenth century*, p.99.
[237] Kirby, Peter: *Child Labour in Britain – 1750-1870*, p.98.
[238] Kirby, Peter: *Child Labour in Britain – 1750-1870*, p.119.

6. Political Countermeasures against Child Labour

As already mentioned above the rising social problem of child labour didn't stay concealed from contemporary society and politics. There were several legislations passed by the British government to protect children at work. In fact 'the century that had the most public exploitation of child labour was also the one that saw numerous laws restricting child labour.'[239] Most of the new laws first and foremost affected those industries with the most children visible at work and/or the highest rates of work related accidents.[240] The first legislations to curb child labour were 'The Labour in Cotton Mills Act' (1831), 'The Chimney Sweepers and Chimney Regulation Act' (1840), 'The Mines and Colliery Act' (1842) and 'The Factories Act' (1844) to name but a few. But what were the reasons for so many legislations? Were the newly passed laws not sufficient enough and therefore demanded for further political intervention? As an example for the numerous laws enacted for the sake of the children's protection at work, the following paragraph of this work will deal with the content of The Factories Act of 1844, it's execution by the government and factory owners as well as the question whether it was really effective in terms of an overall improvement of the children's working conditions, wages and work safety.

6.1 The Factories Act of 1844

The Factories Act of 1844 constituted that the youngest age at which children could be employed at a factory was eight years. This is a fact which deserves special mentioning because the new law actually lowered the minimum age of legal employment from formerly nine to eight years, resulting in the employment of even younger children than before. Children between the age of eight and thirteen were required to attend school for three hours each day and their overall working hours were reduced to six and a half per day in contrast to the usual twelve-hour shift of adults which had been applied to them before the new law had been passed.[241] Furthermore, the ages of the children who were about to be employed had to be verified by surgeons. Additionally, inspectors had to visit factories in order to make sure that the owners of the factories adhered to the new law. But the reliance on those inspectors led to the probably most important problem of The Factories Act: there were way too little inspectors for way too many factories which enticed some inspectors to do their jobs very sloppily. There was an overall lack of inspection and supervision which - theoretically - should secure the observation of the law. For instance, some inspectors simply relied upon

---

[239] Frost, Ginger: *Victorian Childhoods*, p.165.
[240] Cf. Frost, Ginger: *Victorian Childhoods*, p.68.
[241] Cf. Kirby, Peter: *Child Labour in Britain – 1750-1870*, p.105.

questionnaires given to the factory owners, instead of visiting and inspecting the factories in question themselves.[242] Also they had little power of law enforcement except from fines, if they really found something amiss. Due to the understaffing of inspectors, they focused largely upon larger, urban manufacturers which directly caused the neglect of smaller or more remote ones. It can be said that the smaller and remote a factory was, the more likely it escaped inspection.[243] Another problem the inspectors were confronted with was the fact, that there were no official means to record the birth dates of children at the time.[244] Law did not require the registrations of birth until 1874[245] so it was difficult to determine the age of the children. Due to that problem surgeons were supposed to examine the children who should be employed in order to decide, whether they were fir for working or not which meant they could only estimate the age of the children. The whole concept of a minimum age for work was further undermined by the children's own parents. In order to get their children employed as early as possible, parents oftentimes showed the surgeons unofficial or falsified certificates of birth or presented them an older sibling on behalf of the actual younger child in question.[246] In addition to these already grave problems, it was very difficult for the inspectors to keep track of the actual working hours of children while they were at work. A common way of avoiding restrictions on working hours was that a child ended a shift in one part of the factory and then went straight to its second shift in another part of the same factory which had already been inspected.[247] Another great disadvantage of The Factories Act of 1844 as well as its predecessors and antecessors was the fact that it focused – as the name already suggests – solely on children working in factories, like 'The Labour in Cotton Mills Act' of 1831 had solely focused on children working in cotton mills. The Factories Act of 1844 entirely left out children who were working in other sectors apart from factories. The three greatest employers of children – agriculture, domestic service and workshops[248] – mostly escaped inspection even though 'the most intractable cases of child labour were those, in which children were employed 'not in large aggregations, but in scattered units'.'[249] Like its antecessor, The Factories Act of 1844 was highly limited – it restricted child labour in certain industries to specific ages and to maximal working hours instead of giving overall guidelines for all working children. So it can be said about The Factories Act of 1844 that it brought only little improvement to the children. Although the minimum-age of employment was established and

---

[242] Cf. Kirby, Peter: *Child Labour in Britain – 1750-1870*, p.106.
[243] Cf. Kirby, Peter: *Child Labour in Britain – 1750-1870*, p.14.
[244] Cf. Kirby, Peter: *Child Labour in Britain – 1750-1870*, p.106.
[245] Cf. Frost, Ginger: *Victorian Childhoods*, p.70.
[246] Cf. Kirby, Peter: *Child Labour in Britain – 1750-1870*, p. 107.
[247] Cf. Kirby, Peter: *Child Labour in Britain – 1750-1870*, p. 108.
[248] Cf. Frost, Ginger: *Victorian Childhoods*, p.58.
[249] Cf. Kirby, Peter: *Child Labour in Britain – 1750-1870*, p.94.

working hours were theoretically restricted, there were various ways to circumvent these obstacles and violations of the act were not infrequent. Employers and sometimes even the children's own parents found ways to employ underage children. But even though the enactment of the law meant no big change for the children at work, it was nonetheless an important step towards the abolition of child labour. Although it had its flaws, it brought the social problem of child labour into the focus of politics and in the public eye and therefore socially important for the protection of children. [250]

---

[250] Kirby, Peter: *Child Labour in Britain – 1750-1870*, p.110.

7. Conclusion

Concluding the results of the previous pages it can be said that working-class childhoods in Victorian England were decisively shorter than those of their richer peers and were primarily determined by taking responsibilities and starting to work regularly at very tender ages. Due to financial deliberations and the urging pressure of low wages and poverty, many parents sent their children to work as soon as possible in order to relief the family's strained financial situation, at least a little. Even worse was the situation for pauper children and orphans who grew up in workhouses since their general influences on their futures were even lesser than those of their peers living with their families and kin. The children's low wages and the new possibilities of modern technology to deploy children at workplaces which formerly needed the strength of grown men made child labour attractive for employers and formed a possibility for their parents to make some extra money for the family exchequer. In addition to the long working hours, the working conditions were not uncommonly harsh and oftentimes outright hazardous for the children's health. Accidents while operating heavy machinery were frequent, as well as work related diseases caused by an unhealthy environment. Scratching a living in the streets as beggars, pick-pockets or prostitutes oftentimes formed the only alternatives for poor children to a life of hard labour and exploitation by cruel masters. But the rising problem of child labour didn't keep undetected during the Victorian Age. Philanthropic endeavors and the intervention of the government by passing laws to protect children brought the practice of child labour into the public focus and started to acknowledge it as what it was: a great social problem. Voices were being raised to curb child labour and to enable working-class children to go to school on a regular basis. Last but not least it were famous contemporary authors like Charles Dickens who were the first who made working-class children, thieves and prostitutes their main characters and criticized the extreme poverty in the cities, child labour, the failing and injustices of the social system and the conditions inside workhouses in their works of fiction. By doing so they raised the public's attention to this particular topic and dared to write about social taboos. While reading novels like 'Oliver Twist' and 'David Copperfield' today, it gets very clear that the issues mentioned by Charles Dickens about 170 years ago, are still relevant and haven't lost their topicality throughout the centuries. Immense poverty, child prostitution and above all child labour are still prevailing problems in poorer and developing countries these days. The reader gradually comprehends and visualizes on an emotional basis what Charles Dickens wanted to achieve with his fictional works and what the British historian E.P. Thompson summarized in the following way: 'The exploitation of little children [...] was one of the most shameful events in our history.'[251]

---

[251] Kirby, Peter: *Child Labour in Britain – 1750-1870*, p.1.

8. List of Literature

Literature:

1. Cruickshank, Marjorie: *Children and Industry - Child health and welfare in North-west textile towns during the nineteenth century*, Manchester University Press, Manchester, 1981.
2. Dickens, Charles: *David Copperfield*, Wordsworth Editions Ltd., Herfortshire, 1992.
3. Dickens, Charles: *Oliver Twist*, Penguin Books, Harmondsworth, 1994.
4. Frost, Ginger Suzanne: *Victorian Childhoods*, Praeger, Westport, 2009.
5. Humphries, Jane: *Childhood and Child Labour in the British Industrial Revolution*, Cambridge University Press, Cambridge, 2010.
6. Kaplan, Fred: *Dickens. A Biography*, Hodder & Stoughton, London, 1988.
7. Kirby, Peter: *Child Labour in Britain, 1750-1870*, Palgrave Macmillan, New York, 2003.
8. Low, Sampson: *Giants of Literature – Dickens*, Arnoldo Mondadori Editore, Milan, 1968.
9. Mee, Jon: *The Cambridge Introduction to Charles Dickens*, Cambridge University Press, Cambridge, 2010.
10. Mitchell, Sally: *Daily Life in Victorian England,* Greenwood Press, Westport, 1996.
11. O'Gorman, Francis (Hg.): *The Cambridge Companion to Victorian Culture*, Cambridge University Press, Cambridge, 2010.
12. Paroissien, David (Hg.)*: A Companion to Charles Dickens*, Blackwell Publishing, Malden Mass, 2008.
13. Paroissien, David; Dickens, Charles: *The Companion to Oliver Twist*, Edinburgh University Press, Edinburgh, 1992.
14. Peck, John (Hg.): *David Copperfield and Hard times: Charles Dickens*, Macmillan Press, New York, 1995.
15. Shore, Heather: *Artful Dodgers. Youth and Crime in early Nineteenth-century London,* Royal Historical Society/Boydell Press, Rochester, 1999.
16. Steinbach, Susie L.: *Understanding the Victorians. Politics, culture, and society in nineteenth-century Britain,* Routledge, London, 2012.
17. Strange, K. H.: *Climbing Boys. A study of Sweeps' Apprentices, 1773-1875,* Allison & Busby, New York, 1982.
18. Sutherland, John: *The Longman Companion to Victorian Fiction*, 2nd Edition, Harlow, England, New York: Pearson Longman, 2009.
19. Tosh, John: *A Man's Place – Masculinity and the Middle-Class Home in Victorian England*, Yale University Press, New Haven, 1999.
20. Tucker, Herbert F. (Hg.): *A Companion to Victorian Literature & Culture*, Blackwell Publishers, Malden Mass, 1999.
21. Wilson, Angus: *The World of Charles Dickens*, Penguin Books, Harmondsworth, 1972.

Internet sources:
22. Cody, David: *Child Labour*, http://www.victorianweb.org/history/hist.8.html, accessed on 31st of August 2013 at 12 a.m.